YOU ARE SOUND

Resources by Maalii Magdalene Bey

Services

Mini Sound Readings

SoulPath Frequency Readings

1:1 Sound Healing Embodiment Sessions

SoundingMoonSouls ~ A Space for the Divine Feminine

SoundingVeins ~- A Space for Earthians to sing again!

SoundPriestess Mystery Bootcamp & School™ (starting in May 2022)

www.soundingsouls.com

Online Courses - Workshops - Masterclasses

Intensive Chakra-Sound-Healing Workshop

Blossoming Business - 6 Week Coaching program

The Divine Masculine, the Divine Feminine & Your Inner Child

Anxiety & your Voice - plugging into a higher Power Grid

Saraswati Workshop - Tapping into the Divine Feminine

(For more info, please visit www.soundingsouls.com)

Social Media ~ SoundMessages & SoundTeachings

Maalii's YouTube, 'SoundingSouls ~ Maalii Magdalene'

Maalii's Telegram Channel,"SoundingSouls"

Maalii's Facebook Page, 'SoundingSouls'

Maalii's Instagram, "SoundingSouls"

Sign up for Maalii's Newsletter

www.soundingsouls.com

YOU ARE SOUND

Decoding your Divine Vibration

Maalii Magdalene Bey

Printed by Amazon Self-Publishing - First Printing, December 2020

The author of this book does not allocate medical advice or prescribe the use of any technique as a form of treatment for physical, emotional, or medical problems without the advice of a physician, either directly or indirectly. The intention of the author is merely to offer information of general nature to support one's individual journey of spiritual awakening. In the event, you use any of the information in this book for yourself, the author assumes no responsibility for your actions.

Cover Design: Photo edit and Cover design by Magdalene Reich

Cover Photo: by Pixabay, Pexels, licensed by CCO (Creative Commons Zero). The photo of this cover has been dedicated by Pixabay to the public domain by waiving all of his or her rights to the work worldwide under copyright law, including all related and neighboring rights, to the extent allowed by law.

Paperback ISBN:9798535211770
Imprint: Published by Kindle Direct Publishing

Dedicated to the Mother and her Song.

Table of Contents

Foreword by Brigitte Jakob

I came to know Maalii Magdalene when she attended my yoga class at The University of Mozarteum in Salzburg some years ago. She was a young radiant student, curious and full of expectations about yoga. And now only a few years later, because of her spiritual development and life's journey, she is writing a spiritual book. How great is that?

So, welcome to a spiritual quest into sound and silence, into understanding yourself and the universe. I do not see the two, the human being and the surrounding world, as something separate, but connected. Some time ago I came across the following words: "Three seconds after the Big Bang, approximately fifteen billion years ago, the Almighty paused for an infinitely small moment to let out a silent Hymn, a sigh of deep accomplishment, a release of cosmic proportions. A Hymn that resonates and vibrates, undulates, and procreates across the known universe. And if you listen very hard, the tune will come to you at last. You will rock and you will roll. And you shall connect with your eternal soul." These wise words, which were printed on a Goa-style T-shirt, had a deep impact on me. In a few sentences, they illustrated the tantric myth of creation from pure mind and energy to sound, time, and space, continuously materializing and getting more concrete. From this holistic point of view, the essence of the universe is called 'spanda', which is the pulse of life, the vibration, and the energy that - according to quantum physics - is what comprises light, sound, and material.

This book is based on this philosophy. Maybe that is why it explores such diverse areas and different layers of our existence: physical, psychic, emotional, energetic, spiritual, social, global, environmental, biospherical... What I really value about this book are the many practical exercises, useful theories, and enlightening meditations. Because life is not just about cognitive processing, but also about experiencing and feeling things.

Let Maalii's enthusiasm and drive take you on a marvelous journey. Open up your heart to this young woman's profound wisdom and experience the potential of sound. Then you may find what is already inside, in you.

- Brigitte Jakob, Yoga Instructor, Salzburg Austria

Prelude

July 2021.What a time we live in! Who would have imagined possible what's going on on our planet today only 3 years ago? I began writing this book in the summer of 2019 in the heat of New York City. I first published in December 2020, being in Europe at the time - and today, I need to update this Prelude - today, meaning July 12th, 2021 - again, from amidst the humidity of the Big Apple..

In the first stages of typing this book, I wrote day and night, dedicating myself fully to birthing this lettered baby. I wrote and rewrote and meditated, and prayed, and prayed a little more, went through deep inner healing evoked by the materials of these pages, and recorded Sound Meditations and other videos to support anyone who truly wants to go on a transformative journey into one's

Sounding Divinity. I was so passionate about getting the message of this book out there that I forgot to sleep and eat.

Then fall came, and things slowed down a bit. The universe literally slowed *me* down, including my writing pace, teaching me that all the rich stuff I was sharing needed deeper embodiment in my own life. So I listened and slowed down. My guidance was to spend *an hour of my day in nature* and watch the cycles of Earth, taking in her wisdom like a sponge. As a result, writing this book shifted into a more organic flow I saw present in every flower, tree, and plant of Gaia. *Thank God.* I would be dead by now had I continued at my initial pace..

In February 2020, I sang one last opera production in Kentucky before Covid-19 *"hit"* the planet, a planned evil action, initiated by dark powers at play. A "virus", invented, only to produce a vaxxx that is no vaxxx to start with and was only created to inject harmful nanoparticles into the body and brain, so the world's population could be reduced. You think I am crazy? I thought that kind of thinking was crazy up until a little while ago. I thought these were some crazy conspiracy theories. The problem is that the mainstream media, as well as the major social media platforms, are censoring article after article, post after post, video after video, so you stay a conforming, going-along citizen without asking any critical questions based on your *own* thinking, allowing politicians and so-called "scientists" to control you and tell you what to think - and worse - what to put into your sacred body.

Look up Dr. Rainer Fuellmich, a German-American lawyer, who together with a team of international lawyers investigated this massively, you may want to watch his interview with Dr. Peter McCoullough on bitchute.com - furthermore, you may watch this interview of Dr. David Martin about the shocking origin and decades of planning about the so-called vaxxes. Have a look at the circle of the "5 Docs", one of them the best-selling author and gynecologist, Dr. Christiane Northrup, who speak from a medical perspective of what's going on (available on Dr. Tenpenny's website) - and hear about the thousands and thousands of stories of women having extreme discharge and higher amounts of bleeding during their menstrual cycles, as the vaxxs are attacking the ovaries, as well as other organs. Yes - fertility of the human race is being played with. Yes, people are dying from the vaxxes, even people as healthy and fit as professional athletes, and not just a few of them - and no one speaks of it. Yes, these so-called vaxxes really *are* bio-weapons.

No darkness can ever prevail though. This book is about the unfathomable power of your Sounding Soul. Living in its core will carry you through the madness. Divine Vibration will guide you through. Sounding Source and Sounding Source only buzzing in our vein is what will prevail. Light forces are becoming stronger and stronger on Earth - our planet is preparing for a major shift - and the masses are waking up. You are being called to play your part in this transition - you are here on planet Earth at this pivotal time of human history for a very powerful reason.

It's a dark moment of the age we live in. A manipulated world on all ends – a matrix of slavery and control. And yet – no darkness in Heaven or Earth can ever prevail in the presence of Source. This book is about the unfathomable power of the SoundingSoul. It is about the Divine Vibration you are, exceeding anything you have ever imagined. Living in its truth will carry us through the madness. Divine Vibration will guide us every step of the way. Sounding Source and Sounding Source only buzzing in our veins is what will prevail. Transformation is taking place on Earth – our planet is preparing for a major shift – more and more people are waking up and *you* are being called to play your part in this transition. I believe we all are here on planet Earth at this pivotal time of human history for a very powerful reason. And we'll get to that shortly!

Yet, I believe with all of my heart, that every "crisis" – and may it be an artificially imposed one – holds enormous potential. Potential for awakening; potential for transformation; potential for tapping into one's own genius. Crises – or let's call it chaos' – invites us to look deeply within, reflect, find inspiration, and instead of buying into a victim mentality find victorious ways to stand in our truth, and keep creating.

Whatever is going on in your sector of industry, there are creative solutions *within, within the Soul,* for those who dare to seek. We carry within ourselves a sacred-sounding space, connected to the cosmos, connected to Divine Mind, holding all the answers. There is a potential within - *within you* - that can help you move through this time no matter what your current situation might look like. There are solutions. Soul-based ones. And they all have to do with *getting to know the Divine Vibration of your Soul* that made me write this book. So stay with me so I can share with you how I believe you can tap into your inner sounding sanctuary, holding treasures you can't even imagine. The *Sound of your Soul, the Sound that IS you,* will teach you. It will teach you about everything you need to know to go through this adventure called life.

Let's face it - the world isn't just in crisis since the alleged plandemic - we are deep in a predicament for much, much longer. Corruption, greed, manipulation and control are present everywhere: in our governments; the banking and monetary system; health care; poisoned agriculture and food supplies; 5G and HARP; the press and its propaganda played out through the untamable tool of modern technology, just to name a few. We are facing an increase of mental diseases, depression, and disorientation - wherever we look as individuals or as a global collective - we are standing at major crossroads. Each and everyone of us will have to make a choice: to either serve the Light - or to comply with and thereby serve the camouflaged darkness at play.

More than ever, we are invited to *choose life* and first *remember* and then *decode* our sounding divine identity; the core of our God-given purpose, and join the *great transformation* and awakening taking place in our time. It is my prayer that through this book, you'll remember the Divine Sound that you are - enabling you to understand and live by *the Song of your Soul*, guiding and nourishing you from within every step of the way.

Sounding love to you,
Maali Magdalene

Revised Prelude: July 2021 NYC & Texas, April 2022

Introduction: A sounding Journey

"People say that the Soul, on hearing the Song of creation, entered the body, but in reality, the Soul itself was the Song."
-Hafiz (1320-1390)

What if someone told you that everything in this world, everything that you can see with your eyes, is merely a reflection of the *inner, unseen* world, the realm of the *Soul*? What if you came to realize that inside your very self abides the most incredible beauty - that within yourself are *sounding* breathtaking, shattering, all-encompassing frequencies and that you yourself are part of a huge, mysterious, cosmic performance?

What if what you can see on the outside was not all there is, but the world behind your physical eyes was? What if this inner Soul-space was the reality where the answers and mysteries of life lay hidden? What if you carried *all* there is to know *inside* yourself? Furthermore, what if the life you try to live on the outside cannot - *by default* - be thriving while you make that the primary focus when there is a reality within you, much more powerful and true than anything imaginable on the outside? This book has one purpose, and one purpose alone, and that is to tell you, *there is*. There is a reality *within* that wants to be encountered. There is a reality *within* that wants to be remembered and reactivated. There is a reality within so incredibly powerful it would make you fall from your chair upon full realization. Living life from this immeasurable reality is what this book is about. If you want to make yourself home there, come with me; come with me on a journey to the *Sound within*.

Taking a new book in our hands, we might not know where it will lead us - we haven't read it yet. Maybe you're not sure why you are holding this book in your hands - maybe you're just curious, or you love sound and music as I do, maybe it was some sort of a *gut feeling* that made you get this book. Whatever has brought you here, it isn't a coincidence. You are here for a reason - a sounding, radiating reason much bigger than yourself that you will discover on this journey.

The nature of this book

FOR QUITE SOME TIME, I knew I had to write a book about the transformative and healing powers of Sound, Divine Vibration, and our Soul. First, I resisted. Writing a book meant to step up - step up into a higher level of my potential. I was hiding behind the common self-sabotaging thoughts and all kinds of excuses. English, the language I felt I had to write in, is not my mother tongue and that added to my hesitation. I engaged with all kinds of distraction tactics, presumingly keeping me 'busy', so I would have reasons not to start. But, the inner urge of having to bring to paper my life-changing experiences of Sound and Soul neither seemed to be bothered by my fears nor my distraction tactics - *the inner voice didn't stop calling*. After the first quarter of 2019, I kept on feeling that *now* was the time to write but first, the Universe had to bring a personal crisis into my life - a crisis that forced me to pack my things and go back to New York City - and *write*. Once I started, there was peace. Once I began there was flow. Once I trusted my inner guidance, I felt so good and all matters fell into place.

You have in front of you a summary of my own journey of Decoding my Divine Vibration and remembering day by day that *I am Sound.* This journey that led through many ups and downs with existential crises not only once, shaping and initiating me into ever deeper layers of my sounding Soul. I can truly say that my life has been plowed thoroughly multiple times, irresistibly enticing me to surrender to what I couldn't deny any longer: *We are timeless, divine, sounding, cosmic beings in a physical body* - who have chosen to live fully through the physical experience on planet Earth, including the whole challenging spectrum of emotions, may they be of light or dark nature. We are called to lovingly integrate *all* that life contains and become whole again. We are here to remember and come home - *home into the magnificent, sounding truth of who we are*.

I don't know about you, but when it comes to books, we usually buy them, read them, and then store them on a shelf or our kindle. We check the box of having read yet another book on our list. This one is a bit different. This book wants to be a long-term, practical guide. It takes you through twelve essential phases of remembering the astonishing magnitude of your own Soul's Song touching on the fundamental areas of life. You might come back to certain chapters or stay with one for as long as it feels right to you. The more you can allow yourself to trust your intuition, *taking your time to dive deep*, the better your experience will be.

Twelve cyclical phases

WHEN WE OPEN TO REMEMBERING the Divine Vibration that we are, deep inner healing and empowerment are being evoked. Pain is only possible because we forgot the truth of who we are and exchanged it with littleness. Remembering that we are Divine Sound requires deep inner processes *that can neither be skipped nor rushed.* Therefore, we'll go through *twelve* unique phases, essential for this inner journey.

The sacred number *twelve* appears in many cultures throughout history. There are twelve hours of the day, and twelve of the night. A year has twelve months, the zodiac has twelve signs, there are twelve tribes of Israel. Jesus had twelve apostles. A foot has twelve inches, and there are twelve notes before an octave is full. Anything that is either whole or complete is often associated with the number twelve. Moreover, twelve seems to be a *cyclic* number. Cyclic - because we never stop at the twelfth month - we return to the first one. After Pisces, the twelfth sign in the zodiac, Aries, the first one, will follow for sure. And now, there are twelve phases of this book. By going through them, you'll discover that the life areas we'll look at usually return cyclically - not unlike the twelve months of a year. Life itself is cyclic and so is our inner reality, ever-expanding, and evolving.

The twelve chapters are all representing an important phase of the journey. I encourage you to envision a *beautiful, cosmic spiral* – as we have them in our galaxy – and see yourself traveling cyclically through these twelve phases like visiting twelve different stars or planets. You may want to come back to any of them at any time and it would be natural to do so. Think of life itself - imagine the Earth, the planets, our solar system - everything travels in cycles - everything spins and turns around itself. The Earth performs a humongous cyclic dance around the sun every year - and she does so by turning around her own axis every day! Humans seem to have forgotten the cyclic nature of life - we want things to be linear, much affected by our obsession with economic, linear growth at all costs - we want to have everything instantly – like amazon prime – and we get impatient and angry if certain aspects of life require time and regular cyclic re-visitations. We forget that all ancient cultures were built on solar cycles, celebrating and welcoming *all* aspects of life; darkness and light; ebb and flow; increase and decrease; introversion and extroversion; rage and calm, grief and joy; fiery passion and introspection.

The path of *Decoding your Divine Vibration* is a *cyclic journey.* There is no end to discovering, diving deeper, releasing more and more of the limiting littleness we've accepted on the way, and allowing the truth of who we are to come forth.

Intuitive holistic reading

I WOULD LOVE TO INVITE YOU right now to take a deep breath and open your heart wide. Let your intuition guide you when you read this book. Intuition is our gut feeling. Through it, we are able to perceive in a much deeper way than by our intellect alone. My intention is that the message of this book may speak to your interior, to your heart; to the core of your being. I'm not at all interested in feeding you intellectual concepts. I'm not after more material for your mind to *'think'* about. It is my heart's desire for everyone reading this book to *experience* the sounding realm of the Soul. To *feel* the Sound within. *My deepest wish is for you to get into communication with the Cosmic Song that you are part of and therefore will hear the individual Divine Sound that you are.* I invite you to take a few deep belly breaths with me right now while stepping into *the world behind your eyes*, the realm of the Soul. Sounding Source is waiting to lovingly guide you through the journey of Decoding your Divine Vibration. Maybe you'd like to initiate this path with a *Prayer*:

"Hello dear Soul,
Here I am not knowing fully yet what I have signed up for.
I only know I crave to know who I am, I crave to know my eternal sounding nature.
Please guide me through this journey and help me to keep an open heart led by my intuition.
Let me experience who I am. Let me receive the cosmic sounding truth.
Let me hear the Song of my Soul.
And so it is."

SoundSoulJournal

JOURNALING ABOUT YOUR IMPULSES, emotions, and thoughts while reading will help you to allow and engage in deep, necessary inner processes. To get the most out of it, I encourage you to use the pages prepared for reflection in the last third of the book. It is a *built-in-journal* called the ***SoundSoulJournal***. Throughout the book, you'll find promptings to go deeper with the material we are gonna go through. If you read from a kindle, you can still use the ***SoundSoulJournal*** section and get your own physical journal in addition. These times of reflection will make your journey more impactful for your life. This book wants to help you *embody* the sounding truth you're discovering on this journey. It is not about theoretically skimming about the chapters. This book is a genuine invitation to dive deep within your SoundingSoul that is part of the divine cosmic symphony of Source holding us all together. It wants to break you open for change; it wants to speak to your heart; *it wants to envelope you with the Divine Vibration of Unconditional Love and transform your life forever.*

We can have the most amazing concepts in our minds - as long as we're not living them, they'll have no effect on our lives. Reflecting on the different phases, questions, and practices included in this book will allow the shared material to sink deeper into your being. It is scientifically proven that writing down things with your handwriting saves data differently and more sustainably in the brain.

Once in a while, you'll dive into some practical exercises. Those are there to help you cultivate and strengthen your inner antennas to hear and receive *your sounding nature* so it can moist the soil of your life, turning it into a fertile, fruitful garden. After all, what good is it to have read yet another book if it doesn't transform your life in a positive way? I believe being alive means continuous personal transformation, fueled by a kind of curiosity as a child would have it. New habits, attitudes, thought-forms, and empowering beliefs can only take root if we engage in deep inner reprogramming work, paired with a high dose of self-compassion and patience. So I invite you to consider these promptings of reflection and practice as an invitation for deep self-care, personal growth, and self-love.

Virtual Library

YOU ARE SOUND ~ Decoding Your Divine Vibration comes with a ***Virtual Library*** of some videos available on my Youtube channel *(SoundingSouls ~Malii Magdalene)*. There are SoundMeditations and other short videos correlating with certain aspects of the chapters. Whenever you see the *VIRTUAL LIBRARY,* either click on the link directly leading to the video or if you're reading from a paperback, the easiest way is to type in the video title in the Youtube search bar of my channel.

A spiritual path

DESPITE THE GENERAL TREND of moving away from traditional religion, our craving for purpose, for something that is bigger than ourselves has never stopped. We always had and always will have a deep longing for finding out why we are here and what we are meant to do with our lives. *There simply is a part in ourselves that knows we are much more than this life.* We crave a purpose! We crave deeper meaning. We crave to *decode our Divine Vibration!* I believe there is *universal, cosmic truth,* truth that is engraved in the DNA of our Soul - an inner source of knowing - not somewhere far away that we have to say a hundred prayers to - but a source that's inherently *in* us. That is the kind of truth I am after.

I am not promoting any religion but I love sacred scriptures from all kinds of traditions. I grew up with the stories of the Old Testament and I find they hold incredible wisdom. We will discover some of that in later chapters.

It is my heart's belief that the Cosmic Sound of Source will always find its way to those who want to hear it. If you long for it, it will come and *find you*. If you call upon it you will find it waiting *within*. And you will remember that *you yourself* are that Song ~ that you yourself are *Divine Vibration.*

Let the journey begin.

First Chapter: All is Sound

"Each celestial body, in fact, each and every atom, produces a particular sound on account of its movement, its rhythm or vibration. All these sounds and vibrations form a universal harmony in which each element while having its own function and character, contributes to the whole."
-Pythagoras (569-475 BC)

Everything we can see is *energy*. We hear that a lot but have only touched on the tip of the tip of the tip of the iceberg of what this truly means for our lives. Matter is an illusion our physical eye believes to be real. Quantum physics has proven that solid matter actually does not exist. And in a way that's easy to comprehend: Everything consists of atoms, you do, I do, trees do, planets do. Atoms are based on three different particles: protons, neutrons, and electrons and a lot of space in between. The protons and neutrons make up the center of the atom, while the electrons fly around the outside. An atom *is* energy and therefore *everything* is energy.

What's astonishing is that atoms are producing sound. They are miniature musical instruments, sounding non-stop. In 2014, scientists captured the sound of an atom. Our human ear is unable to hear these frequencies - they sit about twenty octaves above the highest notes on a grand piano - a pitch humans cannot perceive. But nonetheless - atoms *sound*. They all have a particular frequency. Therefore, everything *sounds*! Trees sound, flowers sound, rocks sound, water molecules sound, *YOU sound* - without knowing or doing anything consciously - *you sound*. Simply by your pure existence, *you sound*. Whether you bring your vocal cords into vibration or not - *you are a constantly sounding complex*!

Being part of the Cosmic Song

BECAUSE ALL IS ENERGY, everything in the universe is in constant flow and exchange. Our thoughts are vibrating, sounding energy, too. Measurable energy. Just think how sometimes, all of a sudden a particular person you haven't spoken to in a long time pops up in your mind and you call them just to hear them saying, *"How odd, I was just thinking about you"*. Experiences like that are the natural consequences of the sounding electro magnetics of cause and effect, not coincidences. Coincidences do not exist.

Very soon, humanity will have to expand its common understanding of what we really are and how we function. Thoughts and feelings are powerful. They have energetic power, not unlike electricity. This is why thinking certain thoughts will have the corresponding effects - because they are not actually *just* thoughts that you happen to think in your head. They are energy - and that means, they put things into motion.

Humanity will and is already going through dimensional upgrades. There are powerful truths that have been withheld and long forgotten. Truths that challenge the structures of our modern world that mainly depend on disempowered human beings functioning in a pre-made, degrading, profit-driven machinery. We are instead *meant* to wake up to our magnificent, divine nature. *What we are is powerful, cosmically connected sounding energy. We are dynamic energy-beings capable of far more than we are aware of.* If you are made up of sounding atoms, and I am made of sounding atoms, the stars above our heads are sounding complexes, as well as the rivers, oceans, and all creatures - then we are all together woven into one big sounding cosmic symphony like a magnificent magical web - an endless energetic sound-tapestry woven throughout all galaxies; throughout *all there is*. Finally, we are all plugged into the same Divine Sound - the *Cosmic Song*.

VIRTUAL LIBRARY

There is a Sound Meditation called 'I am part of the Cosmic Song', ready for you to be explored.

SOUNDSOULJOURNAL

Maybe you'd like to journal about your experiences during the Meditation.

Eyes versus Ears

WE CAN CLOSE OUR EYES. We do it every night. For the body to fully relax and recover, we need to close our eyelids - a physical functionality essential for our wellbeing. *Our ears are very different.* When we go to sleep, we close our eyes and slowly drift off. But our ears, well, they stay open, because we *cannot* close our ears. Nature has not equipped the ear with this ability. We cannot stop our ears from hearing. We cannot stop our ears from *receiving*. We can't *not* hear as much as we might try. You could say, "Well, I can stuff a pair of earplugs in my ears." Of course, that is true. We can block out some of the decibels reaching our eardrums, but we still receive the sounds that surround us, including the sound of our own breath and heartbeat.

Twenty First century human beings perceive the world primarily through what they can *see*. We look at things and make our judgment. The human eye is based on high-speed light-waves, reflecting from an object and entering the eye. The photoreceptors then convert light into electrochemical signals which when transmitted to the brain are converted as *"seen"*. That way, we decode images all day long. With our eyes, we kind of 'hunt' the events of our lives like prey - our sight lasers its way through them. It's even in the language we use. Our eyes can *"penetrate"* each other - we say *"we see through someone"* - we can kind of *"stab"* someone with our eyes. In short: the eye could be considered a *masculine* organ.

Can we stab someone with our ears? Can we penetrate each other with our ears? What a weird thought! The ear is no organ of penetration. It does not rely on light-waves. It is an organ of *reception.* In German, *auricle* is *"Ohrmuschel",* which literally translated means 'ear *shell.*' A shell is very receptive, taking in anything it is exposed to, like water or sand. Our ears do not rely on fast-traveling light waves. They receive *sound* waves. If we compare light and sound waves, we learn the following: Both sound and light generate wave motions. Sound requires a solid, liquid, or gaseous medium whereas light travels through empty space. Sound waves cannot travel without a medium, while light can. If you want, Sound is the more *personal* wave - it can only exist together with a medium (substance) while light travels through the vast empty space of the cosmos.

With this in mind, it may be an interesting question how our lives would change if we approached it more with our *ears* than our *eyes*. Since the existence of sound is intimately connected to its medium, could it be that the quality of our lives would improve if we paid more attention to *sound* compared to *sight*? Could it be that our experiences, how we relate to others, ourselves, and life in general, would get a whole new feel if we experienced them from the perspective of what we hear rather than what we see? Could it be that we cannot close our ears because sound is inseparably tied to our existence?

You might ask, *"What about the hearing impaired?"* Well, deaf people have the capacity to *feel* vibrations of sound. In fact, hearing-impaired people often learn to communicate by translating different sensations of vibrations through tactile devices. They learn that a certain word has a certain vibrational feeling on their skin and can, therefore, transcribe what has been said. Studies of Dean Shibata, MD. showed that hearing-impaired people are able to sense vibrations in the same part of the brain that others use for hearing. He says: *"The perception of the musical vibrations by the deaf is likely every bit as real as the equivalent sounds, since they are ultimately processed in the same part of the brain."* He even recommends that deaf children should be exposed to music from an early age because the *"music centers in their brain"* clearly get activated and *"may be stimulated to develop."* There is a deep mystery in what sound really is and contains. As much as we are capable to understand sound at this point, its mystery goes far beyond what we can perceive with our physical senses.

SoundSoulJournal:

How would your life be different if you perceived it through your ears versus your eyes?

The Sound of your speaking Voice

IT CAN BE REALLY WEIRD to listen to a recording of one's own voice. Many people have no clue what they're sounding like and are taken much by surprise when they first hear their voices. In everyday life, we aren't necessarily recording ourselves to listen back to how we sound. Of course, we're living in the age of the smartphone and you can easily record yourself and listen to the sound of your own voice. In everyday life though, we need to go with how our voice sounds in our own head and trust the feeling that comes with it. The next time you speak, give some loving attention to what you hear. How does your own voice sound? And maybe more important- how does it *feel* to you? Do you enjoy the sensation, the vibration your own voice generates? Does your voice sound *(and feel)* free or restricted? Is it a warm sound or a cold one? How is it pitched? Rather high or low, or somewhere in the middle? Does it sound earthy, anchored in your body or airy and shy? What underlying emotions can you hear and feel in your own voice? Trust? Fear? Confidence? Joy? Doubt? Excitement? What do you feel you might lack in your interior make-up when examining the sound of your voice? What do you feel you are filled with from within?

I'd love to encourage you to make it a habit and check-in with the sound of your voice once a day. You could do this while having lunch with your family for example; when you're talking to colleagues, or when you are speaking to a friend on the phone. It could be very interesting to observe how you alternate your voice depending on whom you're speaking to or what you're speaking about. How does your voice sound when you talk to your mother or father, your siblings, your partner, or your boss? How does your voice change when you speak about emotionally charged or unresolved material? This exercise is not about judging yourself - it is about increasing awareness. Loving awareness. Awareness with compassion for ourselves. The only way, we change.

Maybe you find yourself not liking your voice all that much - many people do, mostly because on a subconscious level, they know why they sound the way they do. The good news are we can work from both directions. Becoming aware of our interior and healing up is one of them. Working with our voice from the outside is another one. Maybe you'd like to generate more warmth or more relaxedness through your voice if you discover it to be rather stressed, constricted, or shrill. Maybe you feel you need more groundedness - an anchored voice deeply in the body. Maybe you'd like to have more clarity in the way you express yourself and want to develop a confident way to speak so you can be heard. Whatever you might desire to develop concerning your speaking voice, I encourage you to watch the video below, available in your Virtual Library that gives you some ideas on how to work with your voice in a gentle, loving way.

VIRTUAL LIBRARY:
'A guide to a natural, grounded speaking voice' - allowing the Cosmic Sound to move through you.

SoundSoulJournal::
How do you feel about your speaking voice?

You are not a separate unit

EVERYTHING THAT HAPPENS ON OUR PLANET at this very moment has its effect on us, just as everything we create as individuals, has effects on all life. Unfortunately, we have disconnected from the truth of *all being one* to a large extent and mainly see ourselves as little isolated islands. As humans on this planet though, we are intrinsically interwoven and as such must learn how to navigate and honor this truth by taking responsible action that appreciates all life. I believe by *remembering and decoding our Divine Vibration*, which we all carry within us; by realizing who we truly are and acting accordingly, creating harmony, beauty and thereby elevate humanity, our planet has a chance to survive and ascend into high-frequency dimensions we cannot even imagine.

Some time ago, long before the plandemic, I was in a yoga class in Manhattan. The teacher waited patiently for all the participants to settle and then said, *"Let's start this class with the sound of OM, the sound of the universe."* You may think of yoga or *"oming"* whatever you wish, but when everybody in the room, young and old, of different backgrounds, skin colors, and genders joined their voices to *sound* together, it was as if time was standing still. This conscious sound felt like it came from a different plane. I had goosebumps all over my body. We sang it again, this simple syllable, and I felt the sounds coming out of the class' participants literally were plugged into the Song of the Cosmos, holding us all together.

Even if this was just for a moment - it was a powerful experience - one of many experiences that made me write this book. The sound that is in you - the sound that *is* you - is of divine nature and immeasurably powerful. You are here to *sound* yourself into the purpose of your Soul leading to ultimate fulfillment, affecting everyone around you like a ripple effect. You are here to align your life with the vibration of your Soul and follow only that and nothing else. Your Soul's Song is *calling* you. You are meant to get to know it. You are meant to experience it. *Your Soul is Divine Sound. (Your) Sound is a pathway to your Soul. You truly are a sounding Soul; a sacred Song of Divine Vibration.*

SoundSoulJournal:

Do you mostly see yourself as a separate entity from the cosmic, global Whole? If so, where do you feel this perception comes from?

Second Chapter: Sounding Identity Who am I?

"Our Soul sings to us always. If we dare to listen, she will take off the veil of what tries to cover our essence."

Most people when you ask them, *"Who are you?"* will give you answers like: *"I am a doctor"*, or *"I'm Jessica."*, *"I'm the father of two children"*, *"I am a woman"*, *"I am married"*, *"I am a lawyer"*, or maybe, *"I am an introvert."* We often answer the question about our identity with our name, our profession, relationship status, or personality type. But is this really who we are? Our name or our profession? Our gender? Our personality traits? Are these aspects really what defines us as living beings, as inhabitants of the universe? And if not, who or what *does* define who or what we are?

The body clearly is a major part of the human experience, but sooner or later, we all die and leave the body behind. Dying is not evaporating. Dying is *transitioning*. Therefore, it makes no sense at all to limit our identity to the physical. Furthermore, can we be defined by whether we are married, by our relationship status or if we have children? Is our identity tied to being the daughter or son of someone, to belonging to a certain family? Is identity formed by personal success or failure? Most of the time, we won't admit it, but deep down inside us lures a voice telling us frequently we're not enough or that something is inherently wrong with us. Is *that* who we are?

In the previous chapter, we discovered that we must be much more than any of the above; that there is a level of existence going far beyond the physical plane. But who are we then? Could it be that our true nature exceeds everything we can possibly imagine? What if on a Soul-level we are *indefinable*? What if we were powerful, Soul-Beings, that - *consisting of light-filled, sounding atoms* - are supposed to play a unique part in the humongous cosmic symphony?

I love the movie *Avatar*. My favorite part is when Neytiri plugs herself into the magical presence of the trees and connects with them energetically. I love how she communicates with everything alive through senses far beyond what the *'modern, sophisticated'* human being considers possible. How about if Neytiri's reality wasn't just a magical fairy story? What if we actually had the kind of senses she does? What energetic abilities like that were most common in past ancient times and just got lost? What if we were energy-beings, able to sync ourselves with the energetic web of life plugging in whenever and wherever needed - a reality where everything is energetically, tangibly interconnected?

Let's take it a step further - what if in the times to come it were absolutely normal to use these inner, energetic, intuitive, sounding senses - so normal as if we were brushing our teeth or washing our dishes - energetically connecting, communicating, sounding and syncing ourselves with the Cosmic Song; with Sounding Source itself? What if it was already possible to live that way right now?

I AM...

'I am' is maybe one of the most powerful sentences there is. I am. I am. Not because I do but because I am. *I am* - not because I'm married or managed to climb to the top of the career ladder - *I am because I am*. Buddha knew that and so did Jesus whose *"I am-phrases"* reflect a deep rootedness in a sort of identity that's beyond this world. He radiated the Christ Consciousness to an extent that could rise the dead and heal the sick. He embodied his Divine Vibration, inviting us to do the same.

It is said that soon after Buddha's enlightenment a man passed him on the road who was struck by his extraordinary radiance and peaceful presence. The man asked, *"My friend, what are you? Are you a celestial being or a god?" "No,"* said the Buddha. *"Well, then, are you some kind of magician or wizard?"* Again the Buddha answered, *"No." "Are you a man?" "No,"* the Buddha said. *"Well, my friend, then what are you?"* The Buddha replied: *"I am awake."*

What did he mean? He was referring to a state of being - a state that's aware - *aware of an indestructible magnitude within* - he was referring to having remembered his *real* nature - to having heard the Sound of the Soul and recognized oneness with everything there is. He had found the center of being, the peaceful eye of the storm. There truly is a state of being awake - awakening to truth. In an awakened state, we perceive the whole world differently - our previous, disempowered, conditioned system gets an upgrade to its original, divine state, and from that point on, we see the indestructible light of the Soul and hear the all-encompassing presence of the Divine Song in all we encounter.

Awakening to one's Divine Vibration is not reserved for individuals like Jesus or Buddha. Awakening to the powerful Song of Source; the Source of all Life, is a journey available to anyone with an open heart, ready to go on the journey of transformation. Often, the path of awakening includes all kinds of "earthquakes" (crises), shaking up the ordinary, old beliefs around our identity. *It has to.* It has to break up the sense of identity we so vigilantly defend and believe in due to our upbringing, our ideas of how life *should* play out, and the manipulation of the matrix-society we live in. To awaken and truly walk the path of transformation, a solid identity crisis is indispensable. Humans are lazy and as long as we're fairly comfortable, we like to keep things as they are. Without a certain amount of *"earthquakes"* shaking us up, we would feel no need to search for a deeper meaning and purpose to start with.

Identity Exercise

TIME TO DIVE into an exercise to uncover and examine our sense of identity.First, simply fill out the spaces, leaving blank spaces where it says so.

I am *(my name)* Natasha Pavey.
(leave blank) My name does not define me

I am *(my profession)* Artist / Home maker.
(leave blank) My profession is irrelevant.

I am *(my gender)* Female.
(leave blank) I am than the expressed gender in this universe incarnation.

I am *(my age)* 47.
(leave blank) Age is just a number - I am ageless!

I am *(my relationship status)* Married.
(leave blank) The only true relationship I have is with source.

I am *(my nationality)* British.
(leave blank) I am one will all races.

I am *(my skin color)* White.

(leave blank) I defire mysely as one and the same as all on earth + in the unnose.

I am *(an uncomfortable feeling I have about myself)* not Speaking my truth.

always *(leave blank)* I will Speak my truth with ease and grace.

After filling in your answers, read through your list. Have a look through the sentences and just observe how they make you feel. Do these statements make you feel good? Do they give you a feeling of security? Do you maybe feel restricted or claustrophobic? Do the answers make you sad or happy? Why?

Just for a moment, allow the idea of being immeasurably more than what you wrote down on our list. What if your divine identity couldn't be touched by any uncomfortable feeling, experience, or belief about yourself? What if the choices you made in life could never harm who you are on a Soul-level? What if this list had only little to do with who you are? What if being single or in a relationship, being 21 or 55 years old, being a teacher, doctor, lawyer, artist manager - or whatever else you feel defines you - had *no power whatsoever* in the presence of your Soul's divine sounding essence?

Now take your list again and write next to each statement a sentence like this: *'I am much more than xyz'.* Or: *'My identity cannot be touched by xyz'.*

Once you complete your revision, read them aloud to yourself. The revised version could look something like this:

I am much more than the name my parents gave me. In fact, I allow my eternal name to come to me that is not bound by family or generational legacies.

My divine sounding essence cannot be touched by my current profession.

I am more than the expressed gender of this incarnation. The Divine Vibration that is me encompasses the Divine Feminine and the Divine Masculine alike.
My eternal, sounding Soul cannot be limited by age.
My current relationship status has nothing to do with my Divine Identity. I am eternally One with all Life.
My sounding, cosmic nature cannot be limited to any nationality.
The skin color of this or any other incarnation has nothing to do with who I am in truth.
My indestructible, sounding Soul cannot be touched nor harmed by any uncomfortable or negative feeling, belief, or experience.

It is one thing to intellectually agree to the fact that our sounding essence is much more than our limited, superficial definitions. It is one thing to speak of ourselves as being timeless Souls, but it is another to *experience* it. It is one thing to rationally say, *'of course I am not defined by my relationship status'* but it is another story to truly believe it and not be affected by other people who might think we should be, have or do such and such.

You might think, "*I don't like this exercise, it is making me float in open space where I am undefinable and nothing's left of me. I don't want to be 'nothing'.*" While I understand this response, the truth is quite the opposite. Awakening to *our Divine Vibration* means that we are *gaining* - we are truly awakening to Life in its essence, we are waking up to our own and everyone else's radiating divinity, directly plugged into sounding Source. There is no state on Earth richer than that.

Let's continue with our list, this time negating the first statements.

- **I am N O T my name**

How can a name define me? My parents or someone else chose a name, and that was nice of them, but that is not who I *am*.

- **I am N O T my profession.**

Maybe you're thinking, *'I've worked so hard to get my career going - does all the effort not give me the right to claim this as my identity?'* Let's say, tomorrow you had an accident and couldn't commit any longer to your current career. Would you then still like to be defined by it? You *chose* to work in a certain field, hopefully, aligned with what you believe in and are passionate about, but your profession can never define nor fully express your divine-sounding essence.

- **I am N O T my gender as society defines it**

Life exists because of the eternal dance of the feminine and the masculine. We all carry both polarities inside of us. There is a deeper level of who we *really* are, a level of identity that goes far beyond our gender or sexual orientation.

- **I am N O T my age.**

Time is an illusion in and of itself that was forced upon the spheres we live in. Returning to our divine vibrational state diffuses many of the simulated laws currently installed on our planet. To say *'we are not our age'* though, is equally not about denying that our bodies undergo certain changes over time. In fact, there is a lot of wisdom and beauty in consciously growing older (and hopefully wiser) and we would do ourselves good to embrace and honor the natural cycles of life. And yet, on a deeper level - age is an illusion. How can a Soul - vibrating divinity - have an age defined by a calendar that didn't even exist some thousands of years ago? One day, we die, leaving our physical bodies behind - only that dying isn't a full stop, it is a colon. Dying is a transition into another sphere. One day we were born into this physical experience, and if we remember it or not, our Soul signed up for it. For that reason, we are here. We die, and our bodies return to the soil of the Earth and decompose - but our Souls live on -allowing the cosmic, sounding cycles to unfold - however and wherever they want to manifest next.

- **I am N O T my nationality nor my race or skin color**

Whether you love the country you were born in or not; the fact is - your true identity is not dependent on it. While I believe in giving back to our communities and being responsible, active, discerning, and mature inhabitants of planet Earth, our passport has little to do with the depth of our Soul. Our nationality may have left its imprints on certain aspects of our lives, but that is the conditioned self. As children of this cosmos, one tiny nationality of the current world we live in is simply too little to box us up.

- **I am N O T the uncomfortable/negative emotions, beliefs or feelings I might have about myself - nor am I definable by any of the experiences I might have had**

This one is a tough cookie because negative emotions, painful experiences, or limiting beliefs about ourselves usually are rooted deeply in our psyche, often engraved into us from an early age. There is hope though in how we can gently and lovingly tend to those beliefs, transform them, and heal. We do so by deeply connecting with the inner, wounded part of ourselves, being with it, and loving it unconditionally until that part starts feeling safe and we can bring it back home into wholeness again. We will dive deeper into inner healing and transforming limiting beliefs in chapter 4.

For now, maybe you'd like to write down the *'I am statements'* in the negated version yourself. There is space in your journal. After you've done so, come up with a sentence after each statement that comes closest to your inner essence. For example:

I am not my name. → I was named

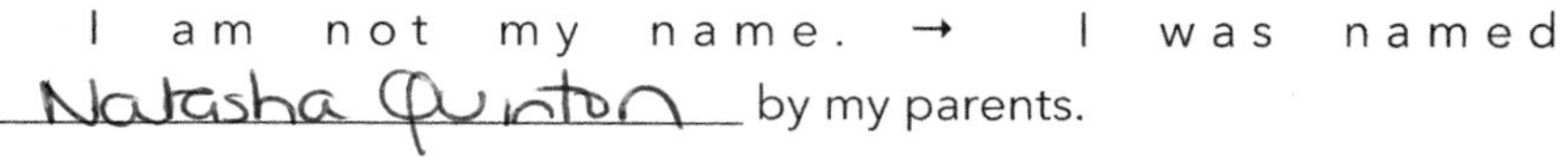

________________ by my parents.

I am not my profession → I chose to work as________________ at this given moment.

I am not my gender → In this lifetime, I was born as Female but I carry the Feminine and Masculine principle alike..

Through this exercise, you can maybe see how we let outside sources define our sense of identity. It wants to help to let go of the old stories we have of ourselves that don't really serve us at all. The list of attributes that seemingly describe our identity are of course much longer. Maybe you see yourself as a funny, very intelligent, extroverted, shy, warm, or driven person. You might say, *'I am a bookworm,' 'I am a very social person,' 'I am a party girl' - 'I am a networker,' 'I am a visionary'* or *'I am an entrepreneur.'* You might feel closely connected to ideas of being a pioneer, a leader, or an artist. I certainly resonate with some of these archetypes. And the truth is, *our Divine Vibration is not faceless*, just as Sound is not soundless - meaning, of course, there are traits and characteristics unique to you in this lifetime.

It is time though, to get to know your Soul's *core*, its *Song,* its *Sound*. If we're cluttered with all kinds of ideas and concepts about ourselves, we will have a hard time hearing it. There is a deeper level of identity than what we allow ourselves to be - there is an inner, sounding magnitude that is our home eternally because *all is one* and the Divine has taken residency within us. Our true nature is plugged into the Cosmic Song, a song of unconditional love that expands eternally and knows no limits.

Our Soul is unremittingly trying to make us aware of this inner-sounding beauty, but because we decided to pay more attention to the noise on the *outside* and to what society tells us we are, we are stuck in a victim mentality; belittling ourselves and others. The key lies in softening and allowing. We can do that by gently speaking to that which is within: *'Dear Soul of mine, I am longing to remember who I am. I want to remember my divine, sounding essence. Please reveal to me who I truly am.'*

Our Soul sings to us always, of that I am sure of. If we dare to listen, she (the Soul) will take off the veil of what tries to cover our magnificent, light- and sound-filled cosmic nature.

SoundSoulJournal:

How did your sense of identity shift throughout the Identity Exercise?

Third Chapter: Conscious Silence

"Listening is nothing less than our royal route to the Divine."
-Dr. Alfred A. Tomatis

Spending time in silence. Real silence. Sitting down without an agenda - no reading, no next youtube video, no social media, no devices, no anything - *just listening*, just being. Most people find this tremendously hard and often scary. It is so much easier to numb ourselves with the distractions of our noisy, busy world. And by all means, it is a noisy, busy world. Creating silence can be challenging. There is traffic and neighbors, sirens and airplanes, construction workers, phone calls, maybe children running around in the house, or pets to be cared for

The silence we're after is relative silence. Silence that took care of the sounds we *can* control and lets go of those we can't. It is *inner* silence. There is a space of inner quiet regardless of any outside noise. Going for a deep dive into the world behind our eyes - *into the Soul* - hat is *'conscious silence'.*

We are here to remember the Sound of the Soul - the Song that is sounding in us eternally, containing the purpose and calling of our lives. Without silence; without *shifting our focus* from the outside noise to the inner realm, we will miss out on our inherent divine vibration and waste away the gift of life. This journey of searching for the Song of your Soul is like diving for a most precious pearl. You won't find it by "staying home", sitting on the couch, and hoping someone will knock at the door and deliver the treasure. Searching means adjusting and modifying what's familiar and comfortable to us; it means getting up and going to where we suspect the treasure to be hidden and prepare by cultivating practices that enable us to dive as deep as possible so we may find the pearl; *the divine Sound within*.

Delicious Silence

NOT ALWAYS ARE WE ABLE to immediately access these deeper spheres of the Soul. It can be difficult and requires willful attention to shift our perspective from the outside world to the inner realm. Sometimes, the outer challenges of life feel so overwhelming that we believe by dedicating time to the world within, we lose control. The ego says, *"You can't afford to focus inwardly, no time for that nonsense!"* The truth is if we allowed the Soul to meet us, the outer world with all its challenges would look very different to us. We would experience the peaceful and clearing powers of the Soul - the only grounds to make sound choices for our lives.

Many people though, when we first start practicing conscious silence, feel overwhelmed by what arises. All kinds of emotions bubble up; thousands of thoughts flooding the mind. A human being thinks between 60,000-80,000 thoughts per day. Practicing silence will point it out. Just as it requires practice to learn a new language, conscious silence needs to be practiced, too. The more we practice, the easier it gets.

I want to invite you to a calming and nourishing *exercise* as a step toward conscious silence. It's a breathing exercise. Getting to know breath is key to remembering what the Soul is made of. Observing and deepening our breath *is* conscious silence.

Breathing ourselves into Bliss

YOU CAN DO THIS ANYWHERE, even while driving or on the subway.

Just sit or stand, or lay comfortably. Whatever position you choose, make sure you straighten your spine. This will help the energy to flow more freely. Relax your shoulders. Maybe roll them around a couple of times in one direction and then in the other. Take a deep breath *in,* and a deep breath *out.* And another one in - and maybe even sigh it out this time. Do that one more time. Feel the rising and falling of your belly and chest as you breathe. If you like, place one hand on your heart and the other on your stomach and just feel your breath moving in and out. Simply feel the sensations in your body caused by your inhale and your exhale. What do you feel? Do you sense any tension somewhere in your body? Just breathe and observe.

With your next inhale, send the energy of your breath exactly to where you located any tension. Nothing to change or fight against. Just send it there. And with your next exhale, release. Do it one more time, *'I am breathing into the tension with my inhale, and I let go of the tension with my exhale.'* Repeat for a couple of times.

And then, try this:

I inhale into my shoulders ~ I exhale and let go of all tension.
I inhale into my jaw ~ I exhale and release all muscles.
I inhale into the space between my teeth ~ I exhale and let go of clenching.
I inhale into my neck ~ I exhale and release.
I inhale into my upper back ~ I exhale and let go of any baggage I carry.
I inhale into my heart ~ I exhale, releasing grief and pain.

I inhale into the space under my arms ~ I exhale and let go of intimidation.
I inhale into my ribcage ~ I exhale and let go of fear.
I inhale into my lower belly and back ~ I exhale and release any shame.
I inhale into my sexual organs ~ I exhale and let go.
I inhale into my knees ~ I exhale and release.
I inhale into my feet ~ I exhale and feel the ground supporting me.
I inhale into the space between my eyebrows ~ I let go of any tension.
I inhale into the beauty of this moment ~ I exhale and I smile.

I call this exercise 'breathing yourself into bliss - practice'. Extend it to your own liking. It can be done anywhere! Now we will add on. With your next inhale, we'll add a powerful inner mantra:

Breathing in: I am - *breathing out:* the sounding Soul
Breathing in: I am - *breathing out:* the Light Divine
Breathing in: I am - breathing out: Love
Breathing in: I am - breathing out: Will
Breathing in: I am - *breathing out:* Divine Vibration & perfect Design.

Breathe through this mantra one more time. This time, especially pay attention to the quality of your breath. Is it short and flat? Can you allow yourself to breathe into the depth of your belly and let your breath expand throughout your body? Is your inhale as long as your exhale? Just observe. How does your whole body feel after this exercise? How do you feel emotionally?

You may repeat this practice as many times as you like with eyes closed or open. *Conscious breathing* is healing medicine for anxiety or feeling ungrounded and insecure. It brings you right back to your center and into the present moment. This inner center of peace is not an imagined fantasy. It is right there, inherently anchored in your being.

Just imagine how your day might look if it started with a few minutes of *conscious breathing,* generating a feeling of connectedness to your center, being relaxed, present, and clear. You could consciously breathe every time you're driving your car, are commuting in the subway, or boiling the kettle for a cup of tea. Making a habit out of conscious breathing by saying to yourself: *'Every time I'm in the elevator, (or stand in line, take a shower, clean my dishes, or sit on the toilet :)) I will use the time given to consciously breathe.'* - or: *'While I am commuting, I will close my eyes for 5 minutes and focus on deepening my breath.'*

Breath is Life

BREATHING IS THE FIRST THING WE DO when we enter this world, and it is the last thing we do before we exit our bodies. Without breath, we aren't able to stay alive for very long. Breath is our life elixir. Surprisingly, we almost never pay attention to our breath. We put so much effort into how we look, what clothes we wear, how others perceive us - and almost *none* into the quality of our breath. This shall not be so.

Creating awareness around our breath is essential to access the space within - the spheres in which the Soul is at home. *Breath* is a doorway to the Soul. It opens up a path leading directly to the Sound within. It rises and falls like the waves of the ocean. It carries messages about the universe, the multitudes of galaxies, the path of our Soul and the mystery of life itself. What might your breath be trying to tell you right now?

Taking a seat behind noise and clutter

BY SURRENDERING to conscious silence with exercises like the one above, we create space. The inner reality has not much to do with all the outside noise of our busy lives. Our essence is *behind* the everyday noise; our essence lays in the realm of the Soul in which we can recharge, rest, and find clarity, and inspiration. Imagine a beautiful throne inside your Soul-temple. That space behind the veil of every-day life, far away from outer noise and mind-clutter, is where your Soul's Song is being sung. It is in that inner chamber where your Divine Vibration is waiting to be received.

SoundSoulJournal:

Let's practice some silence right now! Turn off all devices, sit with awareness of your spine, feel the ground beneath your feet and breathe. Deeply. Count on 4 on your inhale and count on 4 on your exhale. Pause in between in-& exhale for a moment. Do this for 5 minutes.

Outlined in the SoundSoullJournal is a 7 day challenge for practicing silence and evaluating your experiences.

Fourth Chapter: What inside you is longing to be heard?

'The root-cause of painful loops'

'Whatever we have stored away because it is too painful will arise once we commit to conscious silence. It wants to be seen. It wants to be heard. It wants to heal.' - *Maalii Magdalene Bey*

We all carry within an inner child. This inner child, once innocent and pure, has been slowly but surely manipulated into "what works in this world". Initially, it came into the world open-hearted, and free of judgment. Initially, it wanted nothing but to be loved and to love. Originally, the child had one focus - to explore life with curiosity and learn - a little bit more every day. But then, the programming kicked in. The conditioning. The *"This is not appropriate"*, the *"Don't-do-this-and-don't-do-that"*, the *"We-don't-say-these-things"*, the *"Don't-not-be-so-loud"* rules came in. The *"We-don't-talk-about-these-things-in-this-family",* the *"How-dare-you-to-dream?"*, the *"Who-do-you-think-you-are"*-statements. As children, we depend on our primal caregivers. As children, we instinctively know that our parents feed us and give us shelter; our survival depends on them and they are setting the standards. These standards might be good or bad, a mix of collective social norms and personal belief systems of the parents. No matter how good or bad the intentions of the parents might be, eventually, the child gives into their set of beliefs; it adapts to what its caregivers, teachers and other authority figures, or extended family members demonstrate. This is, of course, good in many ways. The child learns to speak, and to walk - to be in the world. That's the one side of the coin - the other side is the belief system of the parents gets imprinted deeply into the child's psyche, conditioning it majorly on a subconscious level - and that's mostly not just positive.

The natural, unbiased curiosity of the child becomes restricted, and the flow of life interrupted and contained. Bit by bit, the child is forced to grow a second skin, a second face, a conditioned identity, dishonoring the unique, expansive Soul incarnate through the child.

A child can't discern yet. So if mum and dad have a fight or ongoing conflict, it will start feeling, *"This must be my fault, there is something wrong with me, why else would they fight all the time?"* The sensitivity and open heart of the child goes so far that even a word spoken in a slightly less than kind tone can evoke a sense of discomfort and establish a belief of *"not being enough"*, or of *"losing love, protection, approval, safety"*. A child isn't born thinking, *"Running around and screaming out of joy is a horrible and bad thing that should be prohibited and punished"*. A child doesn't naturally think *"I simply can't sing - others might, but I, I cant."* (because someone dared to say so), or *"I am not creative"*, or *"I should be afraid of life"* or *"If I speak up, I will lose all love and support"*. None of these so called *stories* (belief systems of the conditioned ego self) are part of the Soul - none of it is true. And yet, we take it on. Why? Because the child is innocent and wants nothing but to love and to be loved. It will do anything to keep the approval (mistakenly confused with love) of its parents going.

Becoming aware

BECOMING AWARE OF WHAT THE INNER CHILD is feeling is a major part of the healing journey. Let's say, you get triggered by something in your present life, and all of a sudden you feel really shitty. To find out what's really going on here, you'd first get yourself out of the triggering situation to create some space. Breathe. From there, fully allow what you feel and observe it without judgment. *"Is this a feeling I know?", "Is this a feeling familiar to me, a feeling that I know from an earlier time in my life?",* "What does it remind me of?" Usually memories from our childhood bubble up. Usually, you can trace the emotion you feel to a situation when you were really little. *There it is.* The inner child. Who's feeling what you're feeling isn't really your adult-self alone – it is the inner child who still holds quite a bit of unresolved emotional baggage - and who can blame it! Let it feel what it feels - allow this beautiful child within you to feel whatever it feels and become aware that it feels that way not because of what just happened in your adult life, but because of what happened when you were little. Now, you can ask the question: *"What did these feelings make me believe?", "What did the situation of this memory cause me to believe about myself?", "What belief(s) did I, as a child, take on in response to the experiences I had?"*

Inviting your Soul

And now comes my favorite part. By bringing in your infinite, higher Self, your divine sounding Soul we've talked about already so much in previous chapters, the immortal Soul to which this book is dedicated, in that majestic, cosmic presence, you may ask the question, "Is this true?", "Is it true that I am not enough, is it true that I am not allowed to express myself freely, is it true that I am a victim? Is it true that life is too hard to be taken on?" In the sounding, divine presence of the Soul, you can help the child to choose anew, inviting in and establishing beliefs that are in accordance with your divine vibration, with the expansiveness and immortality of your true nature. "I am the Soul. I am the Light Divine. I am unconditional Love. I am indestructible. Nothing can harm me. I am eternal Sound. I am forever held in the everlasting embrace of God. I was never alone, in fact, my Soul cannot be alone. I was always good enough. I am eternally loved. I, the Soul, am a sounding expression of God." Speak to your inner child, hold it, and help it to build trust again by lifting it up into the wings of the vibration of your Soul's Song.

The Divine Masculine and the Divine Feminine

Your sounding Soul holds both, the Divine Feminine and the Divine Masculine. Sometimes, the inner child will crave a more feminine presence, like a divine mother without agenda; sometimes it will long for a more masculine presence generating a sense of stability, security and divine reassurance. At the beginning of a healing journey, the Soul usually appears to you in the sex you associate with more. After a while though, you'll notice the subtle nuances of both polarities your Soul carries. Invite in what you need. Ask and you shall be given.

Reconnect, Reestablish, Reaffirm, Repeat

AFTER YOU'VE CONNECTED WITH YOUR INNER CHILD; exposing it again and again to the loving truth of your Soul is what's most needed. To help the inner child reprogram his painful, conditioning experiences, loving repetition and re-affirmation are necessary.

For a very long time, the inner child lived according to its wounds and beliefs - meaning, life was reflecting back his thought-forms like a mirror; bringing about situations that are confirming the belief. That's why, as adults, we can find ourselves in seemingly endless loops without understanding why we repeat the same painful pattern over and over again. It is the subconscious belief patterns of the child, repeating themselves until we become aware of the root cause of the loop, bringing in the sounding truth of the Soul, and thereby, *heal*.

The more time we spend in real dialogue with the inner child; helping him to experience the stabilizing, life-generating, unconditional love of the Soul over and over again, the more we are remembering our divine, immortal origin, rewriting the past, creating new neural pathways in the brain and thereby rewiring our entire experience-archive - this time based on the divine frequency of Soul.

SoundSoulJournal:

Maybe you'd like to journal about a situation that recently triggered you. Going through the steps described above will help you to connect with your inner child and come closer to the root cause of why you felt the way you did.

If you have a hard time doing so, maybe it is a great idea to schedule a session with a trusted spiritual Mentor to get in touch with the more hidden parts of your being. My 1:1 SoundHealing Embodiment Sessions are at your disposal as well. Your intuition will show you the way.

Fifth Chapter: The Power of Self-Sounding

"The knower of the mystery of sound knows the mystery of the whole universe." -Hazrat Inayat Khan (1882-1927)

WHen we take in a breath and are pushing the airflow of our to exhale through our closed vocal cords, we produce sound - we are *sounding.* The body is in fact a resonance body; not unlike the resonance body of a beautiful cello, violin, or a double bass. We - *you and I* - are instruments and are not all that much aware of it. We *are* SOUND.

Producing sound with our vocal cords is deeply connected to the mysteries of the Song within. It holds a sacred key to unlocking the Divine Vibration we are. There is an intimate relation between the *inner* and the *outer* sound; comparable to the union of lovers or the inseparable connection of a pregnant woman to her baby. *Body and Soul are one,* and there is a sacred bridge where the two meet. The bridge is sounding. Chanting ancient Mantras, singing shamanic rituals, spontaneous breaking out in song and dance to praise the Creator throughout the ages - *sounding* from the core of your Soul - a deep and mystical treasure lays hidden within.

"Music is the mediator between the life of the senses and the life of the spirit."
-Ludwig van Beethoven (1770-1827)

~

"Each celestial body, in fact, each and every atom, produces a particular sound on account of its movement, its rhythm or vibration. All these sounds and vibrations form a universal harmony in which each element while having its own function and character, contributes to the whole."
-Pythagoras (569-475 BC)

I love Pythagoras. In school, we learn about him in geometry class - and yet he was so much more than that, knowing that physical and universal sound; audible sound and the Sound of Spirit are all the same; plugged into the ONE sounding Source of all

What we've lost

MOST PEOPLE GET TIMID when it comes to singing - at least when it is about singing in front of other people. *"Oh no, I just sing in the shower,"* is what you might say while blushing. Another common very unfortunate misconception is, *"I can't sing."* With everything in mind we have been discovering together already, I would love to say *that this is simply impossible!* You saying, *'I can't sing,'* is you saying, *'I do not exist.'* How about that?

Especially in the western world, we have fallen for a common misconception of what singing, what *'sounding'* really is. As soon as we feel we don't belong to the category of society's definition of a professional singer, someone who sings for a living, we say, 'Well, I don't belong to this group of talented people,' and 'I will never be able to sing' - end of story. The social engineering imprinted into the matrix we live in has banished natural, spontaneous human expressions through sound, singing and song. We need to understand how this happened. At all times, humans have expressed themselves through ritualistic song and dance. It seems to be in the DNA of our innermost spontaneous interaction with life. Throughout the ages, rituals of song, dance, and rhythm marked special events in life. Birth, death, marriage, entering adulthood, harvest, solstices, equinoxes, new moons, full moons, and so on. Those sounding rituals were a nurturing source of connection. Connection to the Divine as well as to one another. It was equally a healthy way of processing and expressing emotions, experiencing the interconnectedness of all life. Sounding rituals were an expression of the goodness and hardship of life - naturally including all aspects of our being – mind, Soul, *and* body.

Even if we go back in time only a couple hundred years, singing was an established element in society, and family life. *People sang.* They sang together and they sang a lot on all kinds of occasions. In churches, at community gatherings, while hiking, down from the mountains and down in the valleys. Modern manipulated society decided there was no need for a spontaneous song, no use for rituals. *I wonder why.* We got robbed. And bought into the bullshit of social programming, disconnecting us more and more every day from the natural flow of life. We let ourselves be led to believe it was silly to dance or sing for the pure joy of it. We allowed every creative form of expression to be turned into a business that only opens its doors for a pre-selected, so-called 'talented' group. Slowly but surely, we marked creative, spontaneous self-expression as primitive and ridiculous, unless, of course, it was coming from *'a pro'.'*

Don't get me wrong: I am a passionate musician. I was practicing and having lessons for years and years - I still do. The problem is, by putting creativity on a seemingly unreachable pedestal, we have allowed ourselves to be stripped of our birthright to sound, to dance, to creatively express - cutting the vein connecting us directly to the Soul.

It's not a coincidence that we are dealing with an immeasurable increase of depression and mental illness. Did we truly believe eliminating our basic, most natural need for self-expression and connection to the Divine through Sound wasn't gonna leave us wounded, confused and disoriented?

Taking back what's ours

You can sound because you are Sound. If we would learn how to apply the transformative, sounding forces which are inherent in us, our aching planet would heal. Sound in its purest form has the power to shake, re-order, reset, and heal. It can awaken us to our purpose, to why we are here. It reminds us of our partaking in the cosmic song, sounding high vibrational frequencies of healing to all in need. It's time to take back our power.

Humming

I AM CONSCIOUSLY HUMMING almost non-stop while writing this book. Not the kind of humming when we are bored or do not know what to say. I mean humming that increases awareness for the vibrations created, connecting us with the Sound *within*. With deep, grounding hums, especially our chest, heart space, upper back, rips, throat, neck, forehead, temples, cheeks, jaw, and head are being set into vibrations. Really, the whole body starts vibrating, but in these areas, we feel it the strongest at first. Conscious humming generates a blissful stream of peace and wellbeing - it can feel like meditating with open eyes while allowing the humming vibrations to spread throughout the entire body.

On a day of intense writing, I eventually got up to take a break. For the past three, four hours I had been continuously humming. In the moment of sitting down, I felt an incredibly positive energy stream in and around myself, as if being surrounded by sounding light-filled waves (which I was). My immediate response was wanting to continue with my humming to generate more of this beautiful energy. I would love for you to experience the same. Wanna try?

Take a deep breath in, and a deep breath out. And again, with sealed lips, take in an even deeper breath - and an even deeper breath out while humming on your exhale. It does not matter at all how it sounds. What does matter is that you're sounding. Just keep on breathing in deeply and exhale while humming on any kind of pitch that feels comfortable to you. Long deep breaths in - long hums out.

Keep on going and feel where your body is vibrating. Can you sense the gentle buzzing in your body? Keep on breathing in deeply and 'hum out' lusciously as long as you like. You can close your eyes or leave them open. Inhale deeply, exhale, and hum. Inhale into your belly, exhale, and hum.

If you like, place one of your hands on your chest and hum. Breathe in. Hum. Feel. Place your hand on your neck and hum a few times. Inhale. Hum. Move your hands towards your jaw and hum. Breathe in. Hum and observe. How about your forehead? Your temples? Your chest? Inhale and 'hum-hale'. How about your collarbone? Your cheekbones? Just o b s e r v e. How do you feel?

This exercise can be done anywhere, anytime. Just like conscious breathing, it has a grounding, soothing effect. Consciously generating sound with your own vocal cords is like traveling to a deeply nourishing and soothing place of bliss and inner peace.

Now that you are humming, there are no more grounds for the belief, *'I can't sound.'* You can sound. You have just proven it. You just started to reclaim what was always yours: *Universal, cosmic Soundenergy, expressed in the physical through your body*. Keep on humming if it feels good. Hum while you read. Why not? And why not add some conscious humming to your day?

VIRTUAL LIBRARY: (coming soon)

If you'd like some instrumental support, hum with me in the Sound Meditation 'Humming yourself into Bliss.'

OM-ing

'OM' - also *'AUM'* - is said to be the primal sound of the universe. It is a divinely charged, beautiful syllable in Sanskrit, chanted and meditated with for centuries and centuries. It is very similar to syllables of other traditions like 'Hum,' or 'Amen', with linguistic relations. Chanting 'Om' and humming are closely related. When we generate sound through humming and keep our tongue in the same position whilst slightly opening our mouth at the beginning of the sound production, we generate a sound that comes close to the vowel 'A' or *'O'*. By closing our mouth slowly while we keep on resonating, the vowel changes to something more like a 'U' - and at the end the sound transitions to the sensation of an *'M'* through the sealing of our lips. *Try it if you like! Hum, Om, and just feel.*

We can travel endlessly through the transformative spheres of 'Om. It feels like plugging into a higher stream of consciousness, into different, sacred spheres, eternally ringing in the ever-encompassing vibration of SoundingSource. Chanting *OM* is like plugging into the reality that *is* the *real* one (compared to the matrix we live in). You can chant it by yourself, or with a partner, friend, or group. No matter what the setting, chanting 'om' catapults you right into experiencing the cosmic Sound of the universe; it is unifying and self-empowering at the same time.

I began to write this book in the hot New York City summer months of 2019. In the small apartment was one air conditioner only, *not* located in the room I was mostly writing in. From time to time, I would leave my mini kitchen-office, and sit in front of the AC in the other room to break up longer writing phases. I closed my eyes and chanted *AUM* for a few minutes. Now, air conditioners usually make quite a bit of noise - they sound if you like. I felt I was becoming one with the frequency of the air conditioner and we happily *sounded* together. This might sound a bit crazy - but the more we open for the Sound within, we're realizing *and* experiencing (!) more and more that *everything is one*. And nothing is left out by that. *Not even an AC.*

Chanting AUM before important events, before going to sleep, or after waking up will calm your being and bless your day in ways unexpected. Maybe the two videos below can help you explore.

SoundSoulJournal:

Take some time, and explore chanting OM (AUM). If you don't want to do this by yourself, sit down with a friend, or partner, or type in "OM" on youtube and chant along! There are so many videos - just pick what speaks to you spontaneously.

The healing properties of Self-Sounding

MUSIC and SOUND HAVE THE CAPACITY to touch human beings deeply and trigger strong emotions. For thousands of years, music has been used for therapeutic reasons, offering healing energies to all of humanity. I obviously love music and am moved by beautiful sounds all the time; and yet, there is a big difference between being the *receiver* or the *generator*. Being the creator - the sound-source - ourselves, has massive, direct effects on body, mind, and Soul. The Humming and Oming above might have given you a taste of that.

Self-sounding is an embodied pathway to remembering our origin. Sound can feel so comforting to us because it reminds us of where we came from, and where we will go. It reminds us of the unconditional-loving SoundingSource holding the universe together.

The cool part about *'self-sounding'* is: We don't just read about the immortal, powerful, sounding Souls we are, creating another intellectualized concept in our head, but are *physically experiencing* the truth of who we are. With our whole being - our spirit, heart, mind, Soul, *and* body - we are opening ourselves to the power of this truth, healing our fragmented, and often so scattered state of being. Through *self-sounding,* we are engaging in something much bigger than ourselves, joining our voices with the Song of creative Source, and are coming *home*.

~~~

Let me share with you an experience that one of my voice students in NYC recently had

Kasey *(I changed her name to protect her privacy)* has a naturally beautiful voice and loves singing. Like so many, she mostly sings when she is alone. She is comfortable singing in front of a camera recording songs, and sometimes posting one or the other on her social media, but when it comes to singing in front of a live audience, she feels timid. In our first lesson together,I asked Kasey and was quite nervous. I tried to help her see that I was not here to judge her and that it was all about t*hat she allowed herself to sound* - for the joy of it. Period. After a short while, she began to feel more comfortable, and together, we unlocked her voice from being inhibited by the fear of judgment. By creating a space that felt safe to Kasey, her true voice had the space to come through. It was pretty cool to watch - in the course of her very first voice lesson, Kasey found a place of confidence inside herself, a place of deep connection to her truth, from which she began to pull her song outwards through her vocal cords into the world. I was amazed by how quickly she understood how to access her Soul's sound and I could see it by the smile on her face: She had connected with her *authentic* self, the self that doesn't need to copy or impress anyone but reflects the infinity of the Soul. By being vulnerable and opening herself like that for the first time in front of somebody else, she found an element of true inner strength and power, boosting her confidence a great deal.

A few weeks later, Kasey shared with me that she was going through a bit of a rough time when we first started working together. She had experienced a painful breakup, felt depressed, and was going through the many challenges of a young, intelligent woman of our days. Her therapist's advice was to engage in activities she enjoys
~~~

which led her to take singing lessons. I am so glad she did. She told me getting her sound out there made her feel better about herself and gave her strength through this difficult phase of her life.

Sound is powerful. Singing - *self-sounding* - brings the entire body into vibration and helps us to work through fears of all kinds. Singing is healing medicine and very therapeutic. It can change people's lives completely. Singing revolutionized my own life and I'm gonna share with you now how. Ready?

When I was 21, I got accepted by the University of Mozarteum in Salzburg, Austria, as a piano student. Music was always what I wanted to do with my life. I had studied piano from an early age. Although I was very happy to have been accepted into the school, I found myself quite intimidated by other incredibly talented pianists. Students, often younger than me - many of them coming from Eastern Europe, Asia, or Russia - were technically speaking much better pianists than I was, or felt I could ever become. I studied for some years, and enjoyed it - but I always felt that something was missing, that I was not 100% at the right place, not fully in my truth. At some point in my pianistic life, I started to accompany students from the voice department. After working with several singers, I realized that I didn't want to be the accompanying pianist – I wanted to sing. There was such a strong yearning inside that was almost unbearable. I decided to talk to my piano professor about it and she recommended a voice teacher to me. We agreed that whatever happened with my singing, I would finish my master's degree in piano and play my final exam which was coming up soon. We had a deal.

I could not have had a better mentor for my first gentle professional singing steps. A wonderful, amazingly insightful voice teacher. She helped me to feel and experience my body as an instrument. She worked with my whole being, my physical, my emotional, and my psychological setup. She was able to help me face my fears *and* overcome them. She saw my inner blocks through my body language right away and gently made me aware of it. She showed me how Sound was able to transform any fear by singing right *through* it. She had me lying on the floor, feeling my spine supported by the ground, and asked me to breathe from there. She helped me connect with who I am in a much deeper and physical way than I had ever experienced.

Then, I went to London for a few months and studied at the Royal College of Music, officially as a piano accompany student, although singing was all I did. Even my piano teacher started playing for me, coaching my singing experiments. I clearly was addicted to singing, practicing daily for many hours. My teacher there, Amanda Roocroft thought I had potential and encouraged me with her passionate enthusiasm. The feeling of getting over myself; the feeling of my whole body vibrating made me feel so alive and happy that I couldn't stop myself from singing anymore. Something had been seriously unleashed inside and I had a hard time keeping my promise to graduate in piano - a source of sound that now seemed so far away, so far *outside* of me. All I wanted to do was to *sing*!

To make a long story short - I did finish my piano degree - but at the same time, I was already one hundred percent dedicated to pursuing a career as a singer. Something inside me knew I could make it work. Many people called me crazy at the time, asking me why I would start something new again while already (almost) having a degree in piano. I didn't care. I knew I had to follow this voice inside that had woken up and so I did.

Singing changed me as a person. I was often afraid of disappointing people and would rather please others than follow my inner truth. Singing has helped me find my center, strength, and purpose. I am convinced had I not started to professionally sing, I would not be sitting here, writing my first book. While, of course, not everyone is meant to become a professional singer, self-sounding - in whatever shape or form - is one of the most powerful ways to connect to one's inner truth. Self-Sounding helps to overcome fear, it empowers us to step into our full potential and unlocks parts of ourselves that we didn't even know we had. When I first started singing, I couldn't tell *why* singing was so powerful. But now I do. *Sound is SourceEnergy.* Sound is our Soul's *essence*. And if we find a way to reconnect to that ancient, sounding home, we once again are becoming the empowered, light-filled beings we were always meant to be.

Mantras – the power of repeated Sound

MY FIRST ENCOUNTER WITH MANTRAS took place many years ago in a yoga class in Salzburg, Austria. I was in my mid-twenties and had just started practicing yoga, not at all familiar with music featuring mantras in Sanskrit. I was in the middle of a personal transition, a crisis if you want. It was a divorce I went through from a far too early, honestly unwanted marriage in the context of extreme fundamentalistic Christianity. All my so-called "friends" turned their backs on me, including parts of my family. Divorce, that's a no-go in these circles. I didn't care. I knew I was following a pull inside my Soul - and that was definitely NOT to stay in a life that felt like living hell and prison to me. I had packed my very few things and moved back to Austria. I was happy. I was free, only really knowing what I did NOT believe in any longer, but that did not matter either. I knew Divine Intelligence *I* knew; the sounding Source *I experienced* since early childhood was real; was not condemning me at all and would show me the divine plans for my life. So here I was in a yoga class with other music students, trying to open myself to whatever was meant to be …

Gitti, the yoga teacher, had something mysterious and youthful about her - she looked much younger than she was and her eyes were extraordinarily alive and authentic. Her exotic, colorful appearance fascinated me. I was really curious what made her the way she was. In one of the classes, Gitti had us stay in *child's pose* for some time *(a yoga pose where you are on your knees while bringing down your forehead to the ground with arms extended either forward palms facing down or next to your torso, palms facing up)*. In this position, I consciously started to listen to the music that was playing. It was a beautifully sung mantra. I didn't understand a word but all of a sudden I felt deeply moved by the music. Something was gently stroking some forsaken strings of my being. Overwhelmed by a feeling of great compassion and love, I started crying and soon the crying turned into a form of weeping. Deep down from my stomach. I tried not to be noticed by my fellow yoga classmates but my body was shaking. I was so captured by the beauty of the energy rushing through my system that I was lost in the experience and forgot what was around. And then I had one of these aha-moments people talk about. Like a lightning hitting my consciousness. I suddenly understood that all that had happened in my life to this very moment was in perfect harmony and had to happen the way it did, including my momentary crisis. I felt I was loved eternally; I was being held and embraced by sounding Source – I knew that all was well. .

Mantras are sung, repeated phrases of something one could call 'universal truths' as I learned later on. *Om* in and of itself is a mantra. Chanting the same phrase over and over again, one can first think, *'What is the benefit of singing the same thing over and over again*?' Well, you see, mantras are not about long paragraphs of complicated words. Mantras are committed to one phrase, word or syllable that expresses a particular truth. Singing that phrase over and over again is like planting a seed and watering it daily. Mantras can be sounded externally or meditated on inwardly; in either case, they connect us directly to the Sound within, the Sound of the Soul.

Especially the modern western human being often has a hard time doing something seemingly *'insulting'* to the intellect. We easily and arrogantly dismiss traditions and practices that are foreign to us, missing out on their transformative power and wisdom. The meaning of the Sanskrit word *'mantra'* is quite revealing. It consists of the root *'man'*, meaning *'to think'* (also in *'manas'* which means *'mind'*) and the suffix *'-tra,'* meaning *'tools or instruments'* but also *'to liberate.'* A literal translation of the word mantra could, therefore, be *'tools of thought,'* or *'liberation of the mind.'* A mantra has the capacity for profound *transformation*. When we apply a mantra of truth with devoted diligence, it has the power to rewire us inwardly, and set us free.

Bija Mantras - Seed Mantras

IN THE YOGIC TRADITION, our body is divided into several energy centers stacked upon each other, forming a channel from the base of the spine to the crown of our heads and above. These energy centers are called *Chakras*. Each chakra has its distinct characteristics and is associated with certain areas of life. Each energy center saves and stores data. All chakras have a particular mantra, called *Bija* Mantra, *'bija'* meaning *'seed.'* The seed mantras are sounds with one syllable that activate the energy of the chakra, generating balance and harmony. You can chant any of the following seed mantras however it feels right to you. If you need support, just put the Biija Mantra in your youtube search bar and chant along for some minutes, hours or days! ;) *(I mean it)*

The 1st Chakra, also Root-Chakra - In Sanskrit: 'Muladhara' - Seed Mantra: 'Lam'

Our first chakra located at the base of our spine is connected to our foundation. It is called *'root chakra'* or in Sanskrit *'Muladhara'* and governs areas such as our upbringing based on the beliefs of our family/social tribe we grew up in. Muladhara is responsible for our ability to feel safe in the world and have a sense of personal stability and security. If, for example, our primal relationships after our birth were not providing a safe space, we often have an imbalance in our root chakra and can feel generally ungrounded or anxious.

The Seed Mantra for this chakra is *LAM*. Chanting this syllable for an extended period while focusing on our roots enhances healing and brings balance in the areas associated with Muladhara. Singing 'LAM' to the inner child or into early childhood memories can help rewire emotional conditioning and sound healing into what wants to be seen.

For me, there are no rules on how to chant seed mantras. You often hear the seed mantra for Muladhara sung on long extended *L A M S* on lower pitches, but really, chant it as it comes out and see how you feel.

The 2nd Chakra - Sacral-Chakra - In Sanskrit: 'Svadhisthana' - Seed Mantra, 'Vam'

Our second chakra is located below the navel and governs areas such as sexuality, creativity, money, and a sense of personal power. Svadhisthana is the center of creation - it is the energetic and literal womb from which new life is born. The second chakra is associated with the element of water where sensuality, and our ability to experience pleasure are at home. Stiffness, rigidity, or other blockages in the sacral chakra can be the result if creative expression is suppressed. With the seed mantra of Svadhisthana, *'VAM,'* we can balance, enhance, or cleanse the mentioned areas.

The 3rd Chakra - Solar Plexus-Chakra - In Sanskrit: 'Manipura' - Seed Mantra, 'Ram'

The third chakra, also called the Solar Plexus Chakra is located above the navel and around the solar plexus/diaphragm. The element associated with Manipura is fire and often visualized as an inner sun, radiating in all directions. Corresponding life areas are our sense of self-esteem. It is linked to our deeper motivation, and if we are able to follow through with what we committed to. In its mature version, Manipura holds our capacity to be self-sufficient while in reverse it can show submissive tendencies towards another person/ situation/organization. A deficiency of *Manipura* can show in a lack of personal boundaries, a tendency towards lethargy, tiredness, and an incapability to finish what we started. An over-sufficiency of the third chakra is often found in very driven, type-A personalities, workaholics if you want. The balancing seed mantra for the third chakra is *'RAM.'* Try to chant it for a few minutes and see how you feel.

The 4th Chakra - Heart-Chakra - In Sanskrit: 'Anahata' - Seed Mantra, 'Yam'

In the fourth chakra, also called the *heart chakra* or *'Anahata'* we are processing our emotions. Areas of unforgiveness, bitterness but also exceeding joy, being in love and the capacity to deeply and intimately connect with another human are located in the heart. This chakra also is the center of letting go. The biggest challenge of *Anahata* is to keep our hearts open no matter what. Once we close our hearts, life cannot flow through us freely anymore. Many people, after experiencing pain, understandably want to close their hearts. Life, though, is not about not getting hurt - it is about living from the heart, from a vulnerable place, in every regard. Otherwise, we become bitter, dried out river beds missing the purpose of why our sounding soul came here in the first place. Chanting the Seed Mantra *'YAM,'* can help a great deal when it comes to returning to that space of cosmic, unconditional love we originated from - balancing this energetic center of our lives. Give it a try!

The 5th Chakra - Throat-Chakra - in Sanskrit: 'Vishudha' - Seed Mantra, 'Ham'

The fifth chakra, also called *throat chakra,* or *Vishudha,* is the center of self-expression. Vishudha governs communication and our ability to express our truth. It is located in our neck-throat-mouth-area but also includes our ears and capacity to listen. A deficiency of the throat chakra can show in a tiny, almost childlike voice - which is often rooted in the fear of being somehow punished for expressing what we really think. An over-sufficiency instead can be found in people who talk, and talk and talk; people who try to convince others of their point of view with a low capacity to listen. Sometimes, the two go hand in hand. Basically, any kind of uncomfortable sound people produce with their voices originates in an unbalanced Throat Chakra. The deeper beliefs behind these symptoms is what wants to be looked at so it can heal (Chapter 4). *Vishudha* also is an exceedingly creative chakra as we need to somehow verbalize/communicate/voice our creative ideas in one way or another in order to birth them into the world. To balance this chakra, chanting the seed mantra *'HAM' for* at least a few minutes is very powerful.

The 6th Chakra, Third-Eye-Chakra - In Sanskrit: 'Ajna' - Seed Mantra, 'Om'

The sixth chakra also called the Third eye chakra or 'Ajna' in Sanskrit, is located right between our eyebrows. We have an invisible third eye, providing perception beyond ordinary sight. The third eye overcomes duality and reminds us of Trinity-Consciousness - the Holy Trinity which is in all there is. The Father, the Mother, the Child. Our polarized understanding of the outside world (right and left eye) is merging inwardly and activates a higher knowing. Ajna governs our ability to connect with the non-physical and receive divine inspiration. It equally governs our mind and our ability to grasp complicated concepts. Characteristics of an over-sufficiency are overthinking or addiction to rationalizing everything. A deficiency could become apparent in a lack of focus, an inability to concentrate, brain fog, confusion, and depression. Using the balancing seed mantra 'OM' while focusing on the third eye center helps a great deal when it comes to balancing this energetic center. Any form of meditation strengthens the muscles of the Third Eye.

The 7th Chakra, Crown-Chakra - In Sanskrit "Sahasrara" - Seed Mantra, 'Om'

The seventh chakra also called *Crown Chakra* or *'Sahasrara'* is located a few inches above our head, hovering there like a halo. Mystics and saints of all traditions and ages have engaged with the energies of the crown chakra to such a degree that their fellow community members often described them as *glowing*. We still see that phenomena in people who meditate a lot or spend many hours in devoted prayer. Their aura, which is their energetic field, tangibly changes and subconsciously, people are drawn to it like a magnet. The energies of such a human being have been purified, the ego transmuted into the ever-radiating presence of the Soul. *Sahasrara* literally is our channel to connect directly with the Divine; it brings us into the sanctuary of the Soul. Through *Sahasrara*, we remember our cosmic ties. This is where we receive downloads, equipment, and guidance from the higher dimensions our Soul is plugged into.

A deficiency in the crown chakra could be identified in struggling to cultivate stillness - an addiction to doing something at all times. An over-sufficiency can show an inability to deal with practical, everyday life challenges. By focusing on the transcendental spheres of *Sahasrara* only, some people lose connection to practically materialize their Soul's power here on Earth.

To balance Sahasrara, chanting the seed-mantra *'OM'* is very helpful. The seventh chakra invites us to explore the inner, infinite realm of the Soul, connected to the Cosmic Song.

SoundSoulJournal

Did you feel attracted to one or two of the chakras more than to others? What might be the message behind it? Chant their seed mantras regularly for at least a week and journal about your experiences.

The Chakra System & our Energy

THE CHAKRAS are a comprehensive energy model that isn't the primary focus of this book. Understanding them though, is one of the most useful tools for mapping our life's journey. We lose a lot of prana (life force) by having *'energetic leaks'* because no one taught us how to work with our energetic field - meaning, no one taught us how to work with the chakras and keep these life-wheels clear and running.

I've lived the first thirty years of my life without this knowledge and therefore compromised and wasted a lot of my precious life energy. After I gained a deeper understanding of what these energetic centers in my body are I practically worked with what I understood. I systematically examined my life under the magnifying glass of the chakra system. I went through each and every life event where I felt I was leaking energy, calling my energy back into the present time, back into my being, right now, right here. One by one, I cut the energetic cords to old belief systems, painful experiences, memories, *and* people such as ex-partners, family members, or other emotionally charged relationships, and experienced a profound shift. The cord cutting and clearing of my chakras enabled me to let go of situations I felt I never would be. I was suddenly able to let go of people that were absolutely not in alignment with who I am, although before the cord cutting from chakra to chakra, I felt a great deal of an attachment to the person. I can only say, energetic cord cutting works, and bit by bit, I regained the power and strength that always was mine. By doing that, I even experienced *physical* changes. Energy was flowing back in and through my body, making me feel vital again. Some missing parts of me had returned and I felt myself - maybe for the first time. I could write a book in and of itself about the chakras, cord cutting and keeping our energetic centers clear. For now, I'm just gonna say, it works and can help us to shift and align our lives with the sounding purpose of our lives. The chakras function as a map in the realm of the Soul. If you'd like to deepen your understanding of the chakras, Caroline Myss's *'Energy*

Anatomy' and *'Advanced Energy Anatomy'* as well her book *'Anatomy of the Spirit'* might be very helpful resources. Both of these series highly impacted my way of seeing the world, myself, and others.

VIRTUAL LIBRARY - (coming soon)

This short video-guide 'How to call back your Energy - Soul-Retrieval - applying the Chakra system' wants to help you have your full energy available in the now and here. The 'Guided Sound Meditation to call back your Energy.' invites you to work through personal energy leaks and regain what's yours.

SoundSoulJournal:

Maybe you'd like to reflect on energetic leaks you might experience. Which chakras do the leaks correlate with? Would you like to call back your energy and unplug? How could you manage your energy more consciously?

Sacred ancient Mantras of entire phrases

THERE ARE SO MANY POWERFUL MANTRAS you can work with. Om Namah Shivaya. Om Maha Lakshmiyei Namaha. Om Shri Rama, jaya jaya Rama. Om, Eim, Shrim, Chlim, Saraswati Namaha. Om Krim Kalikayai Namaha. Mantras to awaken the Divine Feminine and Masculine; Mantras for abundance and creativity, victory and guidance; death and resurrection. The list is endless. Also here, you can find a lot of support online. Explore those sacred poetic words. They are sounding codes of light, transforming your life. Sing them. Sound them. Chant them. 108 times is recommended.

Your own Mantra

Sound is who you are.

Sound is what brought you here.

Sound is what sustains your life right now.

There is a deep, deep secret in going inward and listening. Listening to that life-bringing Sound of the Soul. Some call it the primal sound. The Sound of eternity. The Sound that is attached to your Soul alone. A sacred syllable containing the frequency for your calling and purpose. What could that syllable be for you? Have you ever sat there in silence and asked? Have you ever sat there in patience and listened until you heard it; until you received this healing sound of truth within your very heart? Each and everyone of us carries within our Soul such a Sound. I have heard it inside. I have heard my name - my *spiritual name* sung to me - and I have heard this one, life-enhancing, nurturing syllable that is mine touching me deeply, transforming every cell of my being. Have you heard yours?

In addition to this sacred, mysterious sounding syllable that is just mine, I almost daily engage with the power of *personalized Mantras.* Sometimes we feel stuck. Sometimes, we are facing certain parts of ourselves that just seem impossible to overcome or simply too painful to heal. A powerful tool can be creating a personal mantra that stands for a truth we'd like to anchor within ourselves. After we lovingly tended to the wounded part inside of us and detected the belief it caused us to have (chapter 4), a mantra replacing the old belief with truth could look like: *"You are infinite and deeply loved. You are enough."* Little phrases such as these sung to yourself, to the wounded part inside, evoke deep healing and transformation.

Neuroscience tells us that it takes repetition to establish new neural pathways in our brains. Different research opinions vary from saying that we need to repeat a newly desired pattern from at least 21 to 60 or even to 90 days. If we have believed certain things about ourselves for most of our lives, it will take some time and patient repetition to rewire the brain, so we can live in the liberating reality of our infinite sounding Soul.

Whatever aspect of truth you would like to establish in your life, creating your own mantra and chanting it is a tremendous catalyst in settling into a new way of seeing yourself, the world, and others. I'd love to encourage you to write a personal mantra in your journal and pin it at various places in your home, where you can see it all the time. Maybe you'd like to have it as a screensaver on your phone and desktop. Seeing it is good, *sounding* it even better. Sing your mantra. Drum it. Dance it. Record it and listen to it again and again. I often record for myself little spontaneous sound messages for my inner *and* outer processes. On my phone's voice memos literally are sounding messages/mantras around inner healing, transformation, abundance, creativity, my calling, and practical things such as aspects of my business, finances, or relationships. When I work one on one with people, I usually encourage the person to do the same - *creating a personal mantra for an inner process that feels appropriate.* Often, we sing and chant together. It is most amazing how singing your own mantra repeatedly, and then re-listening to the recording while singing along massively accelerates inner (and outer) processes of healing and transformation. It is my experience over many decades now, that our being is most receptive to change if we *pair truth with sound*. The reason for that must be that we *are* Sound. Therefore, sounding and singing will beam us right back into the sounding, cosmic reality we once came from, clarifying our Soul's purpose.

SoundSoulJournal:

Have you heard your Soul's sacred syllable? Would you like to sit in meditation and open yourself to receive it?

Additionally, what might be a personalized mantra that would help you transform or heal a certain area of your life right now?

Sixth Chapter: The Song of your Calling

"Your purpose is primarily to be, naturally radiating and sounding your divine, inner nature. To rest in the never-changing ground of being an eternalSoul plugged into cosmic divine consciousness."

Your Soul is constantly sounding, sending messages to you all the time, never ceasing to sing its song. The Soul is forever partaking in the symphony of the Universe, waiting for you to hear and remember it. What syllable did you hear deep inside reading and practicing with chapter 5? The most simple sounds often are the most potent. My syllable, for example, is short, but contains my calling to such a degree that I don't know anything else that would better express the contract of my Soul.

We have never been separate from Source. We have never been separated from the sounding truth of who we are. We have never lost the unconditional love of the Divine. We were always one with the Whole. We carry inside ourselves the frequency of the Divine and the

Divine carries us inside itself. At this moment right now, there is nothing that separates us from cosmic Sound. There is nothing that separates us from the vibration of God.

Entering the spheres of the Soul is like *coming home*. It opens up realities of immortal nature. In these realms within, we use our inner senses, there are *inner* eyes to see, and *inner* ears to hear. We are inherently equipped with these senses. All it takes is going inward regularly, and we'll remember how to use them. Once we glimpse the cosmic beauty within; once we hear the majestic, all-encompassing Song of Source, we won't ever want to live outside this radiance again. *Our journey of awakening has begun*. Awakening to truth and to remembering who we always *were*. More and more each day, we align ourselves with the Sound we heard, realizing that every moment we breathe and live, we have our being in the Sound of Source, calling and pulling us with strings of love. As children run and jump for joy, we run towards the life-bringing tunes of eternity. These Sounds are majestic and oh, so real. *Sounds of Healing and Empowerment. Sounds of expansion and growth. Sounds of bountiful abundance. Sounds of unconditional love.* Sounds overwhelming like a mighty ocean washing us clean from the constructs of our wounded egos. Sounds of hope. Sounds of being part of something far bigger than us. *Sounds of coming home.*

The nature of your Sounding Soul

Sound is *always* communicating a message. Whether we take the sounds of the rain, a beautiful symphony, a crying baby, the sounds of our breath, or of making love, the sounding vibrations of a single atom or the mighty roar of a lion, the sound of the wind or of an erupting volcano – it all transmits this *one message*:

I am!

I AM!

I A M !!!

Being, pure divine existence without condition and judgment, is the core message of all Sound. It is *the* message of creation itself. *I am alive, therefore, I sound - I sound, therefore, I am alive.* A true spiritual path is for us to realize that we *are* - eternally woven into the web of life; it is for us to contribute to that which promotes life. *The Song of the Soul always serves Life.*

When I typed these lines, I placed my head in my hands, realizing that this may be the most important part of this book. Your Soul's Song is always life-promoting; always uplifting; always encouraging, and geared towards blossoming, sacred expansion, serving the Whole. Your Soul doesn't belong to you - it is a fragment of FatherMotherGod, of SoundingSource. The Soul by default cannot be motivated by greed or the illusion of separation. The Soul wants your Divine Vibration to come forth so it can water and transform your life and everything it touches into a beautiful, fertile garden like a mighty river. Your Soul sings to you:

'I AM.
I AM!
I AM!!

I am connected with all life. I am one with every tree.
I am the Divine Consciousness you are looking for.
I am the Guidance within.
I am Cosmic Sound,
I am truth because the Sound of Source runs through my veins.
I am and always will be.
There is no beginning and no end of what I am.
I sound eternally.
I am here to remind you of who you are, beautiful One!
So you may receive the all-encompassing Cosmic Song embracing you with every breath you take.
Remember it. Hear it. Receive it.
It is all you ever were. It is who you are.
You are Love. You are Will. You are Light Divine.

LIFE without end. SOUND without end.
Infinite Expansion.
Cosmic Realization.
Divine Sound is who you are.'

VIRTUAL LIBRARY - coming soon.
The text above is recorded in 'A Message from your Soul' - Guided Sound Meditation. Dive deep into the waters of your endless nature.

Sounding Purpose from within

WHEN THE SOUND OF OUR SOUL awakens us from a deep slumber, change is inevitable. All of a sudden, we hunger for a bigger meaning and purpose. We'll find ourselves questioning trivial elements of our lives, reaching for a higher version of our potential. We slowly wake up from a long sleep and yearn for the radiant, vibrant sounding reality to be present in everything we do. It is time to align our actions, thoughts, words, and belief systems to that which vibrantly rings within - in other words, it is time to disengage with whatever is *not* in alignment with the Song of truth of our Soul.

'What is my purpose and why am I here?', 'What am I supposed to do with my life?', 'What is my mission?' These are questions that have been asked throughout time. We ask them, mostly unaware of carrying the answers *inside* already, looking mistakenly for adequate solutions on the *outside*. We hope our partner will give us a sense of purpose; we unconsciously follow what our parents and their parents consider a fulfilled life to be or want our best friends, career, or boss to give us the key to purpose and meaning. We might go to see wise women or men, psychologists, therapists, doctors, psychics, priests, or shamans so they give us the answer. Throughout time, it echoes: *Why am I here?*

Many people believe purpose is to be found in their *profession*. For some reason, we mix up the question of the purpose with what profession to choose. Just that capacity of the Soul is far too big to be reduced or contained into *one* job. It is much, much more than that. Our profession hopefully is linked to what's alive in us, but it is not the complete picture.

Receiving the Song of your Soul is first about *inner* transformation which will then affect every outer aspect of life. *The process starts inside.* It is initiated by us cultivating a daily relationship with our inner sounding reality. Whenever we try to find purpose and meaning in our lives by starting outside, we might have momentary highs if circumstances are in our favor, but these emotions won't last very long if they are not anchored in the never-changing divine vibration of your Soul.

You are an eternal Soul plugged into cosmic consciousness. You were one with sounding Source before you were born, you are one with it now, and you will be after you're done with this incarnation. *You sound and so you are - and in your cosmic sounding nature lies your purpose and calling.*

A cosmic encounter with your immortal Soul

CLOSE YOUR EYES FOR A MOMENT and just breathe. Just let everything go and listen to your wonderful breath. (I know you're reading) but after you read this paragraph, close your eyes. *Breathe in and hum it out. Breathe in and Om it out.* Do it a few times and just feel. Feel the inner sounding sanctuary within, become aware of your Soul; her rays and waves of light and sound. The Soul carries both, the Divine Feminine and the Divine Masculine and can show itself to you in many ways. She is the inner goddess and the god, the queen, and the king. So receive your Soul now.. Breathing in, and out. Receive your Soul in the way you need it most right now. Receive your sounding Soul in her beauty. For a moment, visualize her as an *inner goddess or god,* forever singing. Let your Soul have a face - let her Song rise inside of you. She *is* you and wants you to get to know all that you are. See her smile and unconditional love. See the instrument she is carrying, gently stroking its strings merging its harmonious sound with her beautiful singing. Hear her laughter. Feel how all is truly well, how you are held in deep compassion. Listen to her Song. *What is She longing to share with you? What sounds or syllables do you hear? By what name is she calling you? Where is she sending her healing song to?*

SoundSoulJournal:

What experience did you make reading through this meditative text of encountering your immortal Soul?

Devotion

PERCEIVING THE MESSAGE of the Sound of our Soul is an ongoing quest of you connecting with you. It won't always be easy as our unhealed parts will try a lot of different strategies to sabotage our inner path. The wounded ego doesn't like the idea of us attuning ourselves with the inner Sound as it disarms the ego's ability to control us.

The unconscious parts of the ego will try to keep us in bitterness, unforgiveness, blame, a victim-mentality, and belittlement. It does not want us to take on responsibility for our own choices and keep us prisoners of our own self-sabotaging patterns. The question is - *who* do we believe? What do we want to build our lives upon? Would we rather live in fear and ongoing pain *or* in the sounding divine presence of Source, holding us forever, equipping us with the resources to heal, become empowered, and blossom into our divine potential?

~~~

Living in the reality of your Sounding Soul isn't easy. It is not easy to go inward while the whole world seems to be concerned mostly with the outside. Devoting your life to SoundingSource takes
~~~

everything you've got. It also gifts you with more eternal wonders you can possibly imagine. We'll get to that in chapter 12. It might not be an easy path to follow to the Song of your Soul; and yet, it is simple. The path is not complicated. It asks one thing of us, and one thing only, and that is our *attention*. Listening to what we hear inside. By surrendering to the Divine Vibration we are, delusive, temporal promises will lose their power over us more and more. Out of the relationship with our Soul will arise clarity about what in particular we might be called to in this incarnation - life-bringing visions deeply rooted in the unconditional sounding love of Divine Source. .

Seventh Chapter: The Song of theBody

Sounding Temple

"We are slowed down sound and light waves, a walking bundle of frequencies tuned to the cosmos. We are souls dressed up in sacred biochemical garments and our bodies are the instruments through which our souls play their music."
- Albert Einstein

For many centuries, religion has demonized the body; industrialization and modern economy ever since abused the body as if it was a machine, and as a result, we are facing severe health conditions. Additionally, the body has long been considered an obstacle on our way to God/enlightenment. Therefore, we are oftentimes disassociated from the innate wisdom of our bodies and function merely guided by our intellect, ignoring the messages of the body. Our economy's "success" is based on this fact; our educational system is, and, unfortunately, also certain forms of unbalanced spirituality are. We made the brain captain of the ship, splitting ourselves into half - head with our intellect - and then the rest of the body that we often treat like a trashcan or slave.

Not always were we so obsessed with the intellect. There were times in human history when there was awareness of the interconnectedness of all aspects of life: our bodies' sensations, our feelings, our thoughts, our metaphysical experiences, our intuition – all was considered as one. Ancient cultures honored and celebrated the body; sensuality; sexuality, and all our physical senses, being well aware of the wisdom anchored in the physical. They were receptive to the sacred whispers of every creek, bee, and branch, embracing the cyclic, all-encompassing nature of life; the archetypal *feminine*.

Unfortunately, through the spread of patriarchal religions, as well as eras such as the Age of Enlightenment, *'I think and, therefore, I am',* we became obsessed with the abilities of our brain. Judaism, Christianity, and Islam are all centering around a God-father-figure in the heavens, far above Mother Earth beneath our feet. Patriarchal, linear systems, with a God that can only be reached through forms of extended mental concentration, were slowly but surely cutting off the body's wisdom; its sensuality, sexuality, and grounded connection to Mother Earth.

There is higher intelligence in our bodies, not just our heads. Scientists, e.g., speak about a second brain located in our belly with major abilities of discernment, healing, and guidance (more about that later).Body hatred has been preached for many centuries. Religions sold the idea of the body being something utterly dangerous, something to be aware of. This caused wounding that is deeply ingrained into the psyche of the collective, even if we see a lot of so-called free-body-expression movements today. The body-programming has wounded humanity on subconscious levels; levels that are often simply suppressed and overwritten by swinging into the other extreme of the pendulum. What's therefore needed is awareness. What does our relationship to our body really feel like? Sitting with whatever arises (chapter 4) and letting it be there without judgment creates awareness. Awareness will create real shifts. And with awareness, healing takes place, reminding us of the divine privilege to live in this sparkling vibrational energy-garment called the human body.

The Divine Vibration of your Soul is not some mystical, esoteric idea floating around in the skies. The Song of your Soul can be experienced right *now*, right *here*, through your body. Remember, sound waves are the ones who can only travel through a *medium*. Sound waves are the *personal* waves, connected to matter. Therefore, to experience the divine sounding reality, we have to get into our bodies. Your Soul decided to live through a body. That's why you incarnated on this planet. Your Soul chose to be on Earth in this form right now. And if the eternal part of us made this choice, who are *we* to neglect the body? Are we not doing ourselves a better service by lovingly tending to our body temples on a daily basis?

We find ourselves expressed through physical form *for a reason*. Every single cell is a sacred set of moving, sounding energy particles, bringing about the most gorgeous temple. Ponder on all the automatic functions of the body for a moment, working for us every single day. The breath, the heart, the lungs, the diaphragm, the liver, the digestive system - all of it operates without our conscious interference. *We are being breathed* - from our first breath until we leave this incarnation. There is divine vibration bouncing back and forth in each and every atom of our bodies. *What is your relationship to your body like? Are there ways in which you could tend to it more lovingly right now?*

Food & Vibration

FOOD IN ITS ESSENCE IS VIBRATION. Living on planet Earth, we need it to fuel the body temple unless you're fully enlightened and can live from oxygen, sunlight, and sound alone. *(I believe we will eventually return to living like this once our original 12 DNA strands have been reactivated.)* As of now though, you probably will need some food to fuel your journey. The quality of what we eat depends on its authenticity; on its vibration - meaning how close the food is to its most natural, original form. Anything we eat has a distinct frequency that can either be in accordance with the vibration of creation - contributing to life and the good of all - *or not.*

Looking at your food choices under this vibrational magnifying glass, what *do* you eat? What do you have for breakfast? What does your average lunch look like? Your dinner? Your snacks in between? And maybe, the most important question: How do you *feel* after eating what you eat? How refreshed, nurtured, good, bad, light, heavy, tired, cranky, bloated, etc., do you feel after certain types of food? Did you ever pay attention to that?

When it comes to nutrition, it is not about *taste* alone. Lots of groceries may taste good at the moment (which depends on what our body is used to), but 20 minutes later, we can feel heavy, tired, lethargic, or maybe even depressed.

The bad news is that lots of so-called foods and what a great percentage of our planet's population puts into their mouths every day are filled with pesticides, poison, and artificial substances that contaminate, weaken, and cloak the body. These substances can lead to severe illnesses, even death. There is a reason for that. Those manipulative forces trying to control our planet want you to eat stuff that is harmful. It is their intention. The more you are disconnected from your divine vibration, the better. The less you are empowered, the better. The more your system is cloaked, the more control they'll have over you, stirring and infusing you with fear - that is and has been their strategy for ages.

Now, to a good extent, the human body stems from Mother Earth. It originated from nature and returns to it when we leave it. Consequently, we are to fill ourselves with fresh, real, authentic foods, directly from Earth. In order to protect our health and well-being, we have to have foods that are life-promoting and were honored *by us* in its organic growing processes.

What will you put in your body every day? Something that has an uplifting vibration because it comes directly from Earth, or something that contaminates your body, full of pesticides, hormones or other harmful artificial substances?

Before I buy certain groceries, I often tune into the vibration. I hold a piece of fruit or vegetable and simply feel. When I walk through an aisle in a supermarket that's packed with artificial, harmful snacks, I feel sick in my stomach. When I walk through an organic farmers market, I feel uplifted and happy. That's not a coincidence. I do the same before I prepare my meals. For example, I love yams and onions. The refreshing layers of an onion. The nourishing sweetness of a cooked yam. I often find myself standing in the kitchen, holding them in my hands feeling their vibration for a while before I cut them up. I sometimes just stand there and listen. Or I say *'thank you, yam, for having grown. Thank you, onion, for carrying inside yourself the wisdom of Mother Gaia. Thank you for serving me now, fueling my body with your beautiful sounding essence.'* I'm not kidding. Cooking is much more fun that way!

Sounding over your Meals

Together with my friend Russell, I sometimes went to a Sikh Temple in Queens, New York City. He is there often and introduced me to how things are done in the temple. After ceremonies, prayers, and lots and lots of singing, everyone eats together. All visitors, young and old, rich, poor, sit on the floor in a huge open space and eat the same meal that has been cooked for hours in a very special way. I was absolutely amazed by the beauty of this community. I learned that day that the temple's kitchen feeds over 3000 souls every day ~ *for free*.

I ate with these loving Sikhs several times and found their vegetarian meals not only very tasty but remarkably different from how I was feeling after the meal, nurtured from the inside out, surrounded by a tangible stream of compassion and love. I felt so good I couldn't explain it at first. It was as if there was a current of love streaming in, from, and all around my body. When I shared with Russell how I was feeling, he told me that the Sikhs start cooking very early in the mornings while *singing* over the food for hours. *'What do they sing?',* I asked. He simply said, *'Love Songs to God, pouring gratitude, love, and appreciation into the food they're cooking."* Now, my extraordinary sense of well-being was no longer a mystery.

Through the beautiful, selfless cooking of the Sikhs, serving thousands of people every day, I had a physical experience of what it means that *all is Sound*; that all is vibration; *that all is one*. I physically felt what can happen when people live this truth and share it with others through the most 'rudimentary' elements of life like our need to eat. The truth is, nothing is rudimentary. The Song of the Divine is vibrating in every aspect of life. Therefore, *eating* becomes a sacred act, honoring and celebrating our wondrous bodies, giving thanks to life, Earth, and sounding Source itself.

Some years ago, I did a 28-day detox-cleanse. The cleanse was based on eating raw organic vegetables and fruit only, starting with a glass of freshly pressed celery juice every day. No oils, no salt, no pepper, no sugar, no coffee. Only raw veggies and fruit, water or tea to successfully flush out all the toxins and heavy metals accumulated in the body. The first week was really hard. Headaches from detoxing. Cravings. All kinds of challenging emotions from detoxing. Hunger. The second week though was already a bit easier and I felt lighter and more energized. Week three was the break-through-week. I woke up early in the mornings with so much energy! *"Yay, another day!!!", "Let's get up and explore!"* was how I felt at 5.00 AM in the mornings! I would never have imagined. One of the days of the cleanse, I was on a two day road trip. I prepared thoroughly and took a huge bag of prepared salads, smoothies and raw veggies and fruit with me. I didn't bring enough though and had to stop at a grocery store on day two. Because the store had nothing organic, I bought some conventional apples, took a bite and stopped. My body was so sensitized at that point and went on strike. I heard a voice inside of me: *"No more chemicals, please! No more chemicals! I cannot take it. You're destroying your own house."*

Becoming aware of the Divine Vibration we are will have effects on our entire life. It does not stop at our food choices. It does not stop anywhere. The Sound of the Soul is cosmic, and yet personal. Hence, I am not here to say there is this *one* right way of nutrition.

What and how we eat is an individual journey and might change over time. However, no matter what nutritional choices we make we are part of the whole. We are meant to be in tune with the Divine Vibration we are, also affecting our food choices. We are the happiest and healthiest if we honor life - our own, that of others, and that of the planet. Many ancient traditions included a *sounding ritual* before meals. There is a reason for that. If it was up to me, I'd love people to sing over their meals before they eat. Singing together a song of gratitude and blessing before we munch away would turn the whole experience into a sacred, celebrational ritual.

SoundSoulJournal:

Maybe you'd like to reflect on your food choices. Do they honor your body, do they honor life? How do you feel after your meals? What would you like to change or explore?

Balancing the Vibration of your Microbiome

MANY STUDIES SHOW IT: Our gut is our second brain. Many illnesses have their root cause in an unbalanced microbiome. A few months ago, I read a book by Dr. Raphael Kellman, called *"The Microbiome Diet"*. It came to my attention through an interview Dr. Christiane Northrup held with Dr. Kellman. I tried what he wrote about, and I felt great. It makes a whole lot of sense and I recommend you read it.

I also tuned in with my sounding Soul and asked my Guides about a year ago to give me some insights and clarity on the subject of nutrition. There is so much out there, and many people say many different things. Maybe you can relate. Truth is, I believe everyone needs to find his or her own truth in this regard. And yet, there are certainly some principles that apply to the human body beyond individual choices. In the following, I'll share with you what I have received from my Soul and Guides. I believe it might leave you with some revolutionary ideas at the least and inspire you to seek out the wisdom of your own Soul at best. Here's what came through:

"The word nu-tri-tion carries the word trinity. The Holy Trinity of the Divine has to be part of what you eat. Anything that has broken up the Trinity of foods and of anything in general is guilty of breaking up the most fundamental law of the universe and will shamefully fail as this can lead to nothing but the opposite of life. Here is an example: GMO foods have broken the holy trilogy of many foods. Corn, e.g., has been modified so many times that it is literally uneatable.

Moreover, humans have such an overindulgence in starks that it is wise to cut them out altogether for several years. This is important especially for people who have been eating a lot of cheap pasta from an early age, as teenagers or in their twenties. Top healthy foods to focus on are Onions, Garlic, and Leek. Asparagus, broccoli, spinach and arugula. Berries. Macadamia and brazil nuts. Have a garden and grow your own organic foods as soon as possible. Celery, cilantro, chives! Oregano, fennel, dill. Cabbage. Radishes of all sorts. Wild herbs. Fruit trees. Banana trees if the climate allows it. Cacao as well!

Avoid refined sugars at all costs. Avoid added artificial flavors - both poison you and create cancer cells. Avoid gluten, avoid starks. Bleached wheat flour is poison. Therefore, no pancakes or waffles that are made with it. No soy beans, no soy based products. Even rice is not the best idea as it is a quite manipulated grain.

Be more creative with your snacks. Master Jesus and Buddha knew what to eat for snacks - they ate what they found in nature. Take them as an example and start snacking on roots like ginger or turmeric, try tiger nuts, dried seaweed, raw cacao. Macadamia nuts and its butter. Use Dandelions, mulberry leaves, mint and nettles for tea.

As for meat - there were times on planet Earth when eating meat was safe and healthy. These times are over. The average meat you can buy in supermarkets based on conventional, worldwide animal breeding is so toxic that you cannot let it into your sacred body temple. No chicken. No beef. No pork. No lamb. Occasionally GAME.

You may eat Game from a trusted source. It is the leanest and healthiest meat you can currently find. Meat is good for grounding a few times a week. Some animals have a contract to be on the planet to help you ground. Leave the guilt trip of pure veganism behind and allow your body's wisdom to tell you what you need once it has been cleansed from its many toxins and linked addictions.

Here's what the controlling forces on the planet are after with their global food agendas: to make you obese. To create more cancer and other diseases so big pharma gains more and more power. To numb you and make you angry. To close your throat chakra. To close Manipura (digestion) as well as your sacral chakra. To uproot you from Mother Earth. To cut you off from Light Source. To paralyze you. To bind you in chains, make you lazy and stuck behind your devices, tied to your housing situation without connection to the Earth, creating more and more depression and suicide. To cut you off from God Source. To dim your light, so you don't want to step into the divine calling of your Soul. To keep you in blind obedience without questioning anything. To keep your brain functioning on a very limited level, far below what it is capable of. To further disable your DNA. To kill you.

Distorted foods make you crave more and more unhealthy foods. Detox! And you'll find that you don't need as much as you have been taught. You need sunlight, tons of clarified water, and the Earth beneath your bare feet."

None of this is meant to scare you - it has to be said though, that the reason why so many people suffer from diseases goes back to extremely low vibrational, poisonous foods that have been manufactured on purpose - to harm you. Take charge of your life and consider your body and health your most precious asset worthy to be invested in.

The effects of Sound on Water

DR. EMOTO, a water researcher from Japan, exposed frozen water to all kinds of different sounds: to classical music, to Heavy Metal, to someone saying *'thank you,'* and to sentences like *'you disgust me'* etc. with quite astonishing results. The water that was exposed to classical music and the appreciative, kind words of *'thank you'* formed beautifully shaped crystals, blossoming into beautiful snowflake-branches that looked like pure art. Whilst the water exposed to Heavy Metal, and mean words showed the deformation of the crystal, breaking down any order, resembling chaos.

The adult human body consists of up to 60 percent water. Taking these experiments into account, we must therefore be highly influenced by the sounds and words we expose ourselves to. Moreover, water is almost as essential for our survival as is oxygen. After learning about Dr. Emoto's experiments, I began to speak kindly, sing, or hum to the water I drink. *'Thank you, water. I love you.'* The waters of the Earth are indeed *alive,* carrying the potential to regenerate our entire planet in the blink of an eye.

(Please be mindful as to only drink distilled or clean spring water. Harmful fluoride and other horrific substances have been added to the main water distributions of most tap water around the planet. Be sure to add some drops of chlorophyll to the water you drink. Fluoride affects our health, fertility, and ability to connect and remember our sounding divinity. It has direct effects on our pineal gland - a gateway to Source - as fluoride calcifies it. There is a reason why the powers trying to control our planet pollute our waters like this. They want our minds to stay in a state of disconnection, confusion, and forgetfulness, as they know, if a Soul taps into her true divine powers, she/he is unstoppable.)

Movement – A Gateway to Soul

A WHILE AGO, I went to an evening of improvisational, ecstatic dance, called *'Wave',* born out of the 5-Rhythms tradition. Over a time frame of about 2 hours, people move and dance around freely with increasing intensity up until a tipping point after which a 'decrescendo' invites the participants to gradually calm and slow down their movements. The experience I had that night was one of the most intense of my life. *I closed my eyes and opened myself to the realm of the Soul. I began to physically express my desires, hopes, and dreams. I danced my prayers* and bit by bit, I was shaking off fear after fear, limitation after limitation – I danced myself free from self-doubts and worry. *Lakshmi*, the archetypal Goddess of abundance and prosperity, was very present for me that night. I felt like I was being showered with beauty and abundance. I knew on a very deep level in my heart that I would never have to worry again about surviving. I had connected with the inherent infinite prosperity of my Soul that knows no lack. I was experiencing the ever-present oneness with overflowing cosmic abundance. I danced with all my heart. I danced wildly and felt the energies of the Earth underneath me, shooting up through the soles of bare feet, anchoring me in *herself*. I could feel the Divine all around and inside of me, realizing *I am Divine Vibration.* It is all I ever was and all I ever will be. *It is all there is.* I was only half-aware of the other people in the room, completely taken by the dimension my Soul had transported me to that night; that I had entered through the gateway of *my body*.

Your body craves movement

It was a gray day in New York City. I stayed in and listened to a spiritual podcast. The interviewer shared how he had lived in a spiritual community in which lots of people committed to a traditional meditation practice lasting several hours each day. They had lived like that for many years, based on the belief that the more one meditates, the more light will be generated, and everything else will resolve and fall into place. While a profound meditation practice is powerful and highly beneficial, the interviewer said, many people in the community struggled with severe health conditions and their bodies were falling apart because they hadn't put any effort into keeping their bodies healthy and strong.

A spiritual path is *not* just sitting down and meditating all day long. Focusing on traditional meditation only is too single-tracked, too focused on the upper chakras only and will lead to compromising *holistic-embodied* transformation. There's a deep calling of our days to let the Divine Vibration of our Soul penetrate *all* aspects of life. It is meant to permeate our relationship to the physical, to being on this planet right now right here, and re-built it where necessary. Our body is a huge part of our experience in this lifetime and the body *loves movement*. We are to experience the joy coming from living in a body that loves to run, and jump, and stretch, and dance - developing and maintaining health, strength, and resilience.

There's no need to become Olympic athletes but we can all do our best to take responsibility for our physical well-being. Our bodies are temples of the Divine. Your body is a dwelling place of God. And that body of yours needs movement. Movement was normal to our ancestors who had to go out to hunt and collect berries and roots to fill their stomachs. In many ways, human beings would be healthier was this still the case.

SoundSoulJournal:

How could you lovingly tend to your body on a daily basis?

Yoga – Holistic Medicine – Moving Meditation

I personally love Yoga. It stretches you. On all levels. It opens your body, mind, and heart - it opens you to yourself, to your sounding Soul. Yoga is moving meditation. It is a beautiful, holistic way to access the divine Song we are. I love it so much because Yoga holds it all at once: meditation, movement, stretching, muscle strengthening, deepening your breath, mindfulness, energy work, chakra balancing, mantra singing, inner peace generating, emotional, spiritual and physical healing, and a general sense of well-being. While there are many different ways in how we can explore the sacredness of the body, I'd love to highlight the benefits of yoga, as it entirely changed my life and is essential on my day-to-day journey.

Yoga is like sacred medicine. It soothes the mind; it can heal emotional trauma; it improves overall health. Yoga cleanses and detoxifies the system. It helps to let go. Through a regular yoga practice, one can access, express, wring, and flush out repressed emotions. Through a regular yoga practice, one can shed that which doesn't serve any longer, may it be inner or outer weight. It allows you to experience little chunks of healing and empowerment day after day.

There are many different types, many different traditions, many different schools. It is up to you to explore and figure out what resonates. Some people love Bikram-Yoga, others prefer Hatha-Yoga, some need their Vinyasa Flow or Kundalini exercises. Experimenting and following your gut feeling will lead to the teacher and style best for you at this very moment. Most types of Yoga are based on ancient traditions containing physical-spiritual wisdom collected for thousands and thousands of years. *Yoga* means *'to yoke' – to bring back into divine union what was always one*. I find that extremely beautiful.

Yoga helps us to develop *a conscious relationship with our bodies*. It is a pathway that bridges body and Soul. I vividly remember how I felt in some of my first yoga classes. I was in my twenties, a bit shy, and worried what others might think of me struggling through the poses – but once I felt the difference yoga made in my life (*I was sleeping better, felt more connected to myself, I became a better musician, I realized a difference in how I was responding to challenging situations and was generally feeling better with less tension in my body)*, my fear was gone and I became a yoga-devotee.

I do yoga every morning - in 2018, I even committed to a 6 months long online yoga teacher training with Ashlee Turner. Not because I wanted to become a yoga teacher - more to deepen my own experience. Yoga has priority in my life before any other tasks of the day. Often, I also end my day with a few yoga poses - releasing any over the day built-up tension. In addition to simply feeling better in my body, yoga has helped me to ground my voice as a singer, gain more confidence in my self-expression and develop a deeper relationship with myself.

In my everyday yoga-practice, I often observe this phenomenon: Before I start, my mind is often all over the place. Sometimes I might be worried about things of the day ahead, sometimes I might feel sad, confused, or am facing a situation where I don't see a solution yet. Once I get into my body, the first thing that happens is that my mind calms down. The dust of my thousands of thoughts and worries settle and I can perceive what actually matters. I often have intuitive impulses while moving my body from pose to pose. I find inspiration and see clearly how I am meant to mold my day ahead. These impulses set the tone for how I structure my time, run my business, and private life. Lots of paragraphs in this book go back to an impulse I had in my morning yoga practice.

As I mentioned before, my yoga journey began in the middle of a life crisis. Yoga didn't only get me through one crisis. I feel since my mid twenties, yoga got me through any difficult time ever since. Yoga and Sound were my anchor that got me through some confusing months and painful stuff in my first couple of years in New York City. I remember certain days, standing in Central Park thinking, *'the only thing that makes sense to me is nature, sound, and yoga. That's it."* Yoga helped me make it 'to the other side'. Without yoga, this book would not exist. Without yoga, I would most likely be a frustrated, bitter young woman that got stuck in the challenges of love and life. Yoga, Sound, nature, and prayer - and sometimes all of them together - are my number one go-tos; my number one medicine *every* day. Yoga helped me hear the Song of my Soul, the Divine Vibration of my Soul's purpose, and calling. *It can do the same for you.*

SoundSoulJournal

Wanna try? :)

Eighth Chapter: The sacred Song of Sexuality

"Lovers have known sometimes what saints have not known."
-Rajneesh

PREFACE: In this chapter, we're looking at Sexuality and related topics. It might evoke a hunger for a deeper sexual experience. Many people have frustration, a feeling of shame, or a sense of unfulfillment around their sexuality. This chapter wants to deal with some of the major wounds and blocks around sex - and also restore hope inside our hearts, how we can find what we are looking for deep within.

I want to separately address those who might have gone through sexual abuse or harassment to seek the help of a professional trusted qualified counselor/therapist. Taking the courage and speaking about your truth can be the first step towards healing. You may also skip this chapter and come back to it at a later time, whenever you feel ready.

~~~
~~~

Sexuality is a sacred gift - a gift of creation - a gift of sacred manifestation - a gift helping us to remember our Divine Vibration. With all our senses, we can experience the pulse of the universe rushing through our veins during love making. Anyone who ever had a real, unfaked, raw orgasm might have experienced how it does not only give you a satisfactory feeling in your sacral area - but a real orgasm can open the heart, the mind, the third eye, and can even lead to mystical, cosmic, consciousness-expanding experiences.

Unfortunately, the collective disassociation from Soul has caused us to forget. We have left behind the core purpose of sexuality and are left with an empty shell. The soulless, superficial, and often harmful sexual standards society advertises, created deep wounding and shame. We no longer live in the holistic knowing of our ancestors of the body, mind and soul being one - and thereby lost the intrinsic treasures of sexuality the universe wanted to gift us with.

Hence, it is time to dive into the mysteries of lovemaking, creating a direct bridge to Soul and Sound: "Divine Vibration of my Soul, here I am with all my longings, wounding, and sexual history. I'm ready for a reset. Speak to me, and reveal what's life-enhancing. Reveal to me the cosmic, sounding sexual riches I have forgotten. Protect my journey with divine grace."

A beautiful and dangerous quest alike. The fires of sexuality have burned many who didn't consider it necessary to understand its deep secrets. We carry lots of shame, misconceptions, and pain around our sexuality that call for our attention. Let's reflect for a moment on the role sex usually plays in our lives. Think about your life choices - *to what locations did you move, what did or didn't you say, what did or didn't you wear, what spontaneous trips did you take, which decisions did you make because of sex?* What we did or didn't do for the sake of seeking out sexual experiences is turning out to be a much longer list than you might have anticipated. Sex drives us. Sex pulls us. Sex is life force. .

We have a deep, raw, wild longing inside our being: the longing for real, passionate union with another. We long for it so much that this inner drive often determines our decisions to a high degree. How many times a day are you asking yourself walking down the streets, *'Am I attractive?'*, *'Am I sexy?'*, or for men: *'Am I good-looking'*, or, *'Did she notice how strong I am?'*

When we experience high levels of sensuality and sexual pleasure, we usually cannot help but *'sound'*, we cannot help but moan and sigh without thinking twice. Whenever we really like something, whenever we experience something as pleasurable or utterly beautiful, our vocal cords start sounding on autopilot. No inhibition, no questions such as *'how will I sound?'* hold us back. Filled with excitement and sensual deliciousness, we're simply expressing our raw emotions. In moments of bliss, our vocal cords don't follow rational, conditioned regulation. In moments of bliss our vocal cords say an internal subconscious "Fuck You" to society's shaming around sounding. In moments of sensual and sexual bliss, we're carried away and our vocal cords sound in accordance with our experience. They express what *is*. They respond to beauty and strength. They respond to pleasure. They finally go along with what nature made them for: *they sound*.

The Divine Vibration of your Soul wants to express itself not only through singing, deeds and actions, but also through your sexuality. Intriguingly, the physical shape of the vocal cords and the visible feminine genitals show visual similarities. Both organs have lips that close and open. Both can receive and give. Breathing in and out, letting prana *(life force)* in and out. Sound is generated when both lips of our vocal cords come together. Life is being conceived when the lips of the vulva are opening and taking in, receiving the semen. Sounding and (sexual) pleasure are intrinsically woven together. They belong to each other like lovers. Throat and Sacral Chakra have a sacred contract with each other, so to speak.

Unfortunately, many people, more often men than women, don't sound while making love. Natural, audible responses to pleasure can be repressed out of many reasons. A fear to *sound*; a fear to make oneself too vulnerable, a fear to open one's heart. By repressing our most natural, audible responses to pleasure, we deny life-force, we deny ourselves the full experience of available life-energy. Why not open your heart and express to the fullest what you feel? It won't only generate more awareness for the Divine Vibration you carry but also create a much more intimate union with your Beloved.

Energetic merging

AS WE DISCOVERED EARLIER, EVERYTHING IS VIBRATION, every cell of the body has its own unique sound. What happens energetically during Sex is this: Two beings vibrating on certain frequencies come together. They start to physically merge and while still radiating their unique vibration, they form a new vibrational composition together - a frequency of their union. In other words: *Two expressions of Divine Vibration, come together and merge.*

The sounding vibrations I am talking about in this book include many different layers of our being - the spiritual, the physical, the emotional, the mental, the energetic, and etheric. The merging when having sex also happens within all these layers. In fact, it happens through each of the energetic centers, the chakras. Because of this, sex is extremely powerful and creates energetic bonds. It can amplify the Soulpower of either partner involved - or dim it. Sex is one of the most intense, beautiful, and risky merging we can expose ourselves to.

Transcending sexual shame

LET'S DIVE INTO AN EXERCISE that will help us to let go of our misconceptions and feelings of shame around our sexuality.

> *Breathe deeply a few times. Breathing in fully, sighing it out completely. And again. Breathe deep into your belly and exhale completely. Now write down any sexual memory that*

feels in any way uncomfortable. Write down anything that arises. What were your family's beliefs around sex? How did your parents speak or didn't speak about it? What were your personal first sexual explorations and encounters? What were your parents' reactions to you discovering your sexuality? Write down anything related to your sexuality that comes to your awareness. Simply be there with any feeling that is bubbling up. Allow it to be felt. Locate in your body where you are sensing the emotion and connect to the part of you that experienced what you remember. What beliefs got created in you in these moments? What are you ready to let go of? (The inner healing processes discussed in chapter 4 are helpful here. - in your ***SoundSoulJournal*** *is room for your reflections)*

Our family of origin & Sex - energetically unplugging from tribal beliefs

Sexual shame often is related to how our family of origin dealt with sex. Was sexuality openly discussed? Was it something no one seemed to be allowed to talk about? Was it played down as something dirty? Did your parents always change the channel when there was a sex-scene on TV? Did you feel safe, encouraged, and supported discovering your own sexuality growing up? What was your experience like having sex for the first time? How did your sexual life develop from that point on?

What I would love you to do is take a deep breath into your *root chakra*, located at the base of your spine, which is where our tribal beliefs are located. What was the message around sexuality in your upbringing? Were thought-forms such as, *'Sex is something dirty'* or *'Self-Pleasuring should make you feel guilty',* or even *'Sex before marriage is sin'* present in your family? Often, when we become young adults, we say to ourselves, *'Well, I don't believe this crap anymore. Now, I do my own thing'.* And maybe you *did* things differently from what your family or primal tribe you grew up in preached as the 'right' way. And yet, our early injections about sexuality often still haunt us and steer our lives from a subconscious level unless we've dealt with their roots. What were your first impressions about what it means to be a woman? What was imprinted in your being about what it means to be a man? Are you comfortable in your own skin? Do you cherish your gender? Do you feel you have a sound, healed relationship to the feminine and masculine principle in general? What even is femininity and masculinity? How does it play out in your life? Trying to create fulfilling sexual experiences and relationships while having deep wounding around the feminine and masculine is like digging a hole in the desert hoping to find an ocean.

Becoming aware of our subconscious beliefs around sexuality is part of the healing. Unplugging from those beliefs is a second step.

Cutting energetic cords to ex-partners

Sexual shame or an uncomfortable feeling can be and often is connected to a person you had a sexual experience with in the past. Unfortunately, school doesn't teach us how to clear our lives energetically and therefore, become able to live fully in the present moment. Vast amounts of our precious energy are all too often still invested in times long gone, tying us to the past. The good news is, we can call back our energy from any person, situation, or system, right now, right here by cutting the energetic cords feeding into the event.

You can do this by engaging in a conscious ritual, literal or visualized, imagining your being consisting of many energetic cords you can feed elements of your lives with. Through these cords, energy is streaming from and also toward you. In the ritual, you focus on the cord(s) still going to past events you do not want to invest your energy in any longer. You may then consciously cut the cords by saying with intention *"I hereby cut the cords to this person and call back my energy. I release this person/situation/event to her own healing path and call back all my power and energy. And so it is."*

This ritual is most effective if you don't just say these words mechanically but pay close attention to your intuition and your body's sensations. To get a thorough clearing of your energetic field, go through all our chakras and claim back the power that's yours, speaking aloud into the unseen world that you're ready to move on; that the sapping energy supply for the old is over. Seal every energetic center with divine protection after cutting and fully unplugging the cord. Archangel Michael is of great assistance in a process like this. Ask him to be there with you. You may repeat this process connected to any ex-partner or sexual situation until you feel a physical, emotional, and energetic shift. (And if you do this from a sincere place, you will.) This is a powerful practice not only in the context of sexuality but to ensure in general that your energetic field is without leak so you can have your life force fully available and present in the *Now.*

SoundSoulJournal & VIRTUAL LIBRARY:

You may use this video 'Calling back your Energy' and its corresponding Sound Meditation as a template any time.

The sacred potential of Sex

Take any masterpiece in this world. Think of the paintings of Michael Angelo in the Sistine Chapel. Would this breathtaking ceiling exist, had Michael Angelo not dedicated years of his life to this comprehensive artistic process? Would any of the great symphonies reach our ears today, had the composers stopped after writing the first ten bars of music? *'I don't want to do this. Too much effort. Too challenging. Let's move on to whatever's next'* (A common modern-day (sexual) attitude).

Think of Rodin's incredible marble statues. Whenever I go to the Metropolitan Museum of Art on 5th Avenue in Manhattan, Rodin's sculptures capture my attention the most. They somehow speak directly to my Soul and touch me on a deep level. The world would be without their astounding depths and beauty, hadn't Rodin committed to a raw piece of marble until the envisioned perfection was coming forth.

When it comes to making love, we believe, we can experience passionate, breath-taking, multi-dimensional sex without devotion to the other, commitment, honest communication about our desires, and *practice*. We're rushing from one partner to the next or content ourselves with the sexual status quo never becoming fully honest, vulnerable, available, present, and open. There's gold in the mine. We just need to dig for it.

Being by Yourself

'What if there is no partner in my life right now?' – you might ask. Surprisingly, deepening the relationship with our sexuality isn't dependent on a partner. Sometimes it can be *essential* to spend time with our sexuality alone. It provides space to heal. Sexual pain and shame inevitably lead to more pain if ignored. Phases of being by ourselves give time to reflect and explore our sexuality, diving deep into sacred sexual spheres we might have never experienced or allowed before. Knowing ourselves sexually generates a depth empowering our lives. A depth any fulfilling (future) partnership, relationship, or sexual encounter highly benefits from.

Who made the law saying we cannot explore our sexual desires by ourselves? Unless you are sexually comfortable with yourself, you won't be comfortable with a partner. A true appreciation for yourself and your body and authentic self-love needs to be practiced and established first.

Society has branded self-pleasuring as something we don't talk (much) about, unless in rather shaming ways. We shy away from speaking about it and see it as inadequate or dirty. Society has reduced sexual-self-care to the mere act of touching and rubbing one's main sexual organs to produce a quick orgasm, cutting out the wide field of sensuality and self-knowledge of the body as such. We are energetic, beings in a physical coat with the capacity to experience deep sensuality and sexual excitement. Some people choose to not have sex. That is an individual choice. Although, *repressing our natural sexual desire* entirely *is neither necessary nor is it healthy.* There is divine beauty in giving *yourself* sexual pleasure. There is bliss in exploring your body, giving it your full presence and attention, and letting it express itself the way it naturally wants to.

Sacred Sexual Self-Care

ON A BEAUTIFUL WINTER DAY some years ago, I very consciously practiced sexual self-care. I lit some candles, prepared some deliciously fragrant oils and began to touch myself gently. I took time to honor and celebrate my body, inviting my Soul's power, in particular the Divine Masculine on that day. I experienced something monumental that afternoon. First, I felt guided to bless all my sexual organs, and realized how much shame was still *"sitting"* in my cells. I allowed myself to feel the pain, cried, and fully felt what was there to feel. I saw where the beliefs came from and brought healing to my inner child. Once I felt a shift and much lighter, my Divine Masculine guided me to deeply breathe, while I continued to touch myself however my body wanted me to. No matter how much I wanted to hold my breath, I kept on breathing deeply. It felt like I was breathing myself slowly into an orgasm; my Divine Feminine and my Masculine making love. It was a challenge at first, as I came close to climaxing and wanted to hold my breath - but I kept breathing, fully and deeply, throughout all my chakras. In and out. Right into the excitement, right into my heart space, right into the infinite Sound of Source within my body. What happened then, is something I had never, ever (!) experienced before. My entire being, every cell of my body seemed to expand and explode simultaneously. I felt vibrating energy firing through my entire system, I felt a volcano had been unleashed, affecting every part of my body - *I had a whole-body orgasm.* Waves were rushing through my body different from anything I had known up until that point. I believe, the energies of the Divine Masculine were tangibly unifying with the Divine Feminine inside of my being, my body *and* my Soul. It was pure ecstasy. My heart was stretched wide open and I felt *one* with sounding Source, one with the world, one with myself. Hours and hours after the orgasm, I still felt it in my body. A feeling of peaceful bliss and relaxation. A feeling of being enveloped in the unconditional love of source. A feeling of a yummy, sensual, divine vibration within every cell of my body.

It felt as if *I had been opened.* Opened into an increased capacity of perceiving sounding Source, my Soul, and everything around myself. This experience changed my life. It changed my perspective on sexuality and my body entirely, proving to me that there isn't a single aspect of life that the Divine Vibration of my Soul doesn't want to touch and extend itself through. In fact, *divine vibration is all there is.*

If you don't have a partner and are longing for one, start with matching the vibration of the partner you want to attract. Start by becoming the man or the woman you truly want to be with. Take responsibility for your life and stop the projection game. Then, call in your soulmate.

Making love – sounding ecstasy

ONE OF THE YUMMIEST THINGS YOU CAN DO with your partner is breathe together. Breathe deeply and slowly in sync with each other while making love. There is a divine law of an eternal flow of giving and receiving between the Divine Feminine and the Divine Masculine. Breathe into each other. Give and Receive. Sometimes, you will play the more receiving role, sometimes you'll be on the giving end no matter what your gender. We carry both, the Divine Feminine and the Divine Masculine within our Souls. The Divine Feminine is giving BY receiving first. The Divine Masculine is receiving BY giving. It is a sacred secret. You may want to receive each other and give yourself from chakra to chakra. Meaning, you together breathe into the root chakra, and with your exhale send energy to the root chakra of yoru partner, then the Third Eye Chakra; the Throat Chakra; the Heart Chakra - going through all those yummy energetic centers one by one. This way, you'll connect with your partner in ways you might have never before. If you keep on breathing deeply and consciously, focusing and sensing the energy exchange between you and your partner, more often than not you will both be facing strong energies of climaxing before even being through with this exercise.

Let your Divine Feminine have sex with the Divine Masculine of your partner. Let your Divine Masculine make love to the Divine Feminine of your Beloved - and all the in between, never forgetting: You are a divine sounding being in a physical body - and so is your partner. The more we see each other from a level of Soul, the more sex becomes a gateway through which we can experience the Divine. In its essence, we are making love to God. And God is making love through us. Through conscious sexuality the physical and non-physical merge into one. We're no longer held by space and time but are opened into a reality much bigger than us. Then, making love will turn into sounding ecstasy. Cosmic, orgasmic Sounding, echoing through the ages.

May our sexuality become a Song of adoration to the Divine,
echoing the truth of our Soul.

Appendix: Channeled poetic Input

"Sex is creation. Sex is union and powerful manifestation if the intention is set right. Sex is connection on all Soul-levels. The Triad. The Monad. The Hierarchy. The Shamballa. The human plane right now. It is all of it simultaneously. It is moving through all galaxies and being right here right now. Only few souls have the maturity and clearing necessary to experience it that way.

The Kingdom of God is amongst us indeed. The Kingdom of God is expanding through Soul-Sex.

From an understanding of Soul sex is to be the following:

Sex is divine power. Sex is divine love. Sex is will. Sex is intention.
Sex is here to create.
Everything.
Sex is play ~ and sex is the most serious endeavor
Sex is fire ~ and sex is water
Sex is earth ~ and sex is Air
Sex is fire ~ and sex is Earth
Sex is Earth ~ and sex is water
Sex is water ~ and sex Air
Sex is Air ~ and is fire.

Sex is all of the above and needs all elements. Sex needs to be infused with the spirit of God. Sex- sacred union - is the spirit of God. Sex is. Sex is creation. Cosmic Sex is what brought about all there is. Twinflames co-creating in the will of God. And where it is out of accordance, it brings harm and poisons. Where it is out of accordance, it destroys.

Always.
There is no room for wiggle here. There is either creation for Soul purpose or creation for low vibration ego purposes. There is nothing in between.

The actual act?

Gentleness is key. Gentleness and stoking the fire with air. Breath. Breathing together. Touching. Gentle touching. Until the water is dripping. Stoking the fire in the body so the water starts boiling.
Hydration is essential. Water. Sacred water taken into the body on the day of union. As much as possible and not so much in the hour before unification.

Gentle strokes. Gentle backs and forth. Gentle.
It will evoke the most extreme passion and tension.
Looking into each other's eyes.
Staring until you lose yourself in your Beloved.

Ninth Chapter: The Song of Gaia

Living in the sacred frequency of the Earth

"Humankind has not woven the web of life. We are but one thread within it. Whatever we do to the web, we do to ourselves. All things are bound together. All things connect." -Chief Seattle

The Earth is filled with splendor. The Earth is filled with grace. The dew of heaven has wetted the planet and it is those who hear Gaia's Song and live in her frequency that are the happy messengers of divine awakening, transformation, abundance and healing.

Unfortunately, the human species is undergoing a dubious development; disassociating ourselves more and more from nature. Depending on what we do for a living, we spend most of our day *indoors*. Modern economy functions like a seemingly unstoppable clock that doesn't leave much room to be outside. Most of us get up, commute to our job, work the entire day, get back into our car or the train, back into our house or apartment, meet friends for dinner - repeating the same routine day after day. What about our fundamental need to be in and with nature?

Originally, the human species evolved from Earth. Our ancestors lived under the open sky. Their everyday life was based upon the cycles of Mother Earth. They ate what nature provided depending on the seasons. They were in awe of the wonder of every sprouting blossom, every ripening fruit. .

We *are* nature, we are not separate from the planet. We are part of it as much as every mountain and plant is. With our modern lives, we have deprived ourselves of the intimate relationship our ancestors naturally had with the Earth. No wonder we are sick. No wonder we're dealing with depression in increasing numbers, no wonder many people face seemingly endless energy-lows.

As we learned earlier in chapter one, the Earth has its own frequency that she is unceasingly sounding into the cosmos. What might her frequency be like? Have you ever felt it? What might her nourishing song be like? Is she crying out for her children to return? Is she raging about the injustice done on her grounds? Is she enticing us to dwell in her riches and splendor?

We are in desperate need of a deep connection to Mother Gaia on a regular basis. If we would follow her call to come back to her and live by her life-bringing cycles, she would cure our many woes. She would cure our heavy hearts. She would lift us out of depression - *she would*. We *are* Earth and if we would only gain back this denied, fundamental aspect of our identity, we would become whole again and find healing for our restless minds.

The Song of your Soul naturally honors Mother Earth. It can't otherwise - unity consciousness, oneness with Earth, is in the DNA of our sounding nature. We need to heal and strengthen the relationship we have with our beautiful, blue planet. We are invited to listen to the wisdom within to find our way back to organic living. We need Soul-centered navigation about what's to be done.

SoundSoulJournal:
How could you reestablish a deep relationship with nature, with Mother Earth?

A love relationship

ONCE UPON A TIME, we had an intimate relationship with Mother Earth - a connection so deep that we felt in total harmony with nature. A connection that was indeed as intense as Neytiri's reality (the main character in the movie *Avatar*). Experiencing harmonious oneness with everything alive, understanding the language of the trees, hearing the song of the flowers. Neytiri is dancing with the butterflies and flying with the dragons. She has a relationship with nature that could be compared to one of two lovers. Passionately attracted to each other. Two being one. Deeply in love, deeply in awe, ready to protect the other with one's own life.

What's your individual relationship to nature, to the Earth? When did you last wholeheartedly spend time outdoors? Listening to what nature is saying to you. Feeling her sounding energies. Tuning in with a river, ocean, or forest. Sensing the birds and bees. Feeling the warm rays of the sun on your skin. Pausing to smell a flower, taking in all her scent. Leaning against a tree and simply listening. Relaxing into his soothing essence. When did you last wholeheartedly breathe in nature's bountiful abundance?

Earth's natural frequency: 432 Hz

The Earth has a natural frequency it resonates in - and that is 432 Hz. We find this frequency in plants and trees, in the ocean and the soil, the crystals and gemstones of the planet. Also the human body naturally vibrates and syncs itself with 432 Hz. We are meant to live in synchronization with the Song of the Earth. You can do that by walking barefoot on the ground, by taking in sunlight or swimming in the ocean or a lake.

Some people can hear the deep vibration of the Earth - it is a deep buzzing hum - the hum of ancient Gaia. It is as healing as it gets. Medicine for free! Sensing the Earth's vibration is a metaphysical experience you can have when tuning in with her. Sometimes, the Song of Gaia can call us to places we have a soul-contract with. Sometimes, the Song of the Earth will tell you where to move or travel to. Sometimes, it will simply heal you. Many of us are called to work with the energies of Mother Earth. If you're one of them, sound will play a major role in this. Sing to the waters, sing to the land; sing to the trees and the air in the sky. Join Gaia in her Song. Ask her to vibrate through your being. It will shift the atmosphere into uplifting energies and bring healing all around.

One thing I've noticed being a musician my entire life is that if people naturally start singing without the accompaniment of an instrument, they usually sing in alignment with the frequency of 432 Hz. There is a reason for that: it is natural to the body!

The manipulative forces on the planet, socially engineering humanity with the intention to enslave and numb us, have set the world tuning of orchestras (and other musical setups) to 440 Hz. This higher pitched, unnatural frequency creates disharmony in the body and increases anxiety, fear, and aggression. It makes you compliant, and prone to manipulation. Shopping malls irrigate the consumer day-in-day-out with manipulative musical 440 HZ noise, also called pop songs, to make you buy and want more and never be satisfied. It is not a surprise that the Nazis played a najor part in the establishing of 440 Hz worldwide - it supports dictatorship and propaganda, control and a system of slavery.

In your everyday life, you might want to pay attention to what frequencies you're exposing yourself to and start listening to music at 432 Hz. If you have instruments you can tune yourself, tune them to 432 Hz. It is not only healing to the body, but will uplift your mood and help you rebalance your system.

Trees - Sounding Friends

It happened for the first time a few years ago. I went for a run in Central Park and stopped under some gigantic, beautiful plane trees. I especially love this kind of tree and there are lots of them in New York City. At the time, I was hitting rocky waters in my life, and only being in nature and doing yoga daily made any sense to me. I stood there and prayed. Under the tree. For guidance. For strength. For hope. The wind was blowing and the leaves danced their dance. All of a sudden, one of the lower branches was bent by the wind and gently stroked my head. I felt an energy stream rushing through my system. *'You are never alone. We are always with you.'* That's what I heard. I stood there, tears streaming down my face. I felt the loving presence of these gigantic beings so strongly, as I had never experienced before. The branches kept on moving in the wind, as if somehow lovingly watching over me, touching my arms and shoulders, face and chest. I couldn't move. I just stood there, crying, taking in all I was feeling. It was as if these trees formed an energetic circle of grace around my being. *They are alive. They sound and they are alive.* This was only the beginning of my relationship with these beautiful, wise giants.

Trees radiate healing frequencies all the time. They communicate with those who dare to listen. Trees are great comforters. They have an incredibly gentle way of lifting our spirits. Wherever I walk, I look for the trees. I thank them. I thank them for being there and sharing their beautiful energies. I thank them for being there even though we pollute the air they have to breathe. Whenever I can, I stop at a tree and I put my hand on its trunk or lean against him. I close my eyes and breathe. I connect to the wonderful, magical being he is. It always soothes my heart and very, very often, I receive the exact inner guidance I need at that moment.

In the process of creating this book, I had a moment where I felt tired and weak. In addition to my commitment to writing (which was already a full-time job), I was launching an online course, conceptualizing a second one, trying to engage with and share my message on social media while teaching lots of private students in NYC and preparing my next opera gig – in short, I was exhausted.

After a call with a mentor of mine, I came to the conclusion that I had to give myself at least two days off to reset. I especially needed time in nature. I decided to spend my mornings down at the Hudson for the rest of the week. The first day, I felt an urge to walk up to a tree I had been at before. I love that tree. It's a mulberry tree with delicious berries in the summertime. Some of his branches hover right over the water. They are strong and can easily carry a person's weight. So I sat on the mulberry tree. Another huge branch was located right above the one I was sitting on and so I could lean my upper body onto the upper branch, completely surrendering my weight to the tree and letting go. I closed my eyes and felt the strength and stability of the tree. I felt his kindness and welcoming energy. I was truly exhausted, and all I could do was absorb. *'You are always welcome here. Come back anytime.'* I started crying - because I genuinely felt the loving energy of the tree. This wasn't made up. This tree spoke to me and was wrapping me in his soothing, grace-filled mantle that day. I was so moved by his unconditional kindness. I cried some more and said "Thank you for being here. Thank you with all of my heart."

For me, walking under trees is like walking under a beautiful green veil of grace. It's the garment of the Mother. It is a tapestry of green, loving abundance the Earth has woven for us. There is sounding wisdom in each rock. There is sounding wisdom in each flower and each drop of water. I believe Mother Earth is continuously singing her Song to us, trying to reach and teach us, sharing her ancient, wholesome knowledge with us. *If we would only listen!* Mother Earth carries the sacred Sound of life inside herself that we need to hear. Many indigenous tribes have received her messages. Some of us still do. It is one of the major callings of our days to return to her Song once more.

Reconnecting with Mother Earth

Standing barefoot on the grass

BAREFOOT. On the grass. On Mother Earth. Gracing her with your feet as if they'd kiss the ground. Feeling her support beneath you. That is a sacred ritual indeed. Try it. Take off your shoes and feel. Simply standing on the grass, on the life-spending soil beneath. BREATHE. Take an inhale and breathe in energy through your feet. You may want to visualize how you are inhaling energy from the Earth into your feet and throughout your chakras, forming a central channel to the crown of your head. With your exhale let go back out into the atmosphere that which does not serve you anymore. Let go of the idea of being separate from the Earth beneath your feet. Let it go. Sink into her. Feel your oneness with her. Let all misconceptions and overly intellectualized mind traps dissolve and decompose. Realize that you, indeed, are the Earth, nurtured by her life-spending energies.

Feeling nature with our bare feet is truly a grounding, sacred practice - available to us at any time. I remember two years ago, I took a bus to Boston to see a friend performing with an opera company. I was early and so I decided to do some yoga after my long bus ride in the Boston Common, a park in the middle of town. It was fabulous. I took off my shoes, my blazer, and necklace and stood barefoot on a sacred mat *made of grass*. For a longer time than usual, I stayed in a pose called pigeon pose where one's forehead touches the ground - in my case that day, *the grass*. I visualized an energetic cord from the space between my eyebrows *(the Third Eye Chakra)* going directly into the ground. I was breathing deeply, connecting to Mother Earth, letting go of the accumulated stress from traveling. I so enjoyed this surrendering practice and felt as fresh as a daisy afterwards,

One can also do this laying on the tummy, visualizing an energetic cord from the belly button going deep into the ground connecting you to the nourishing energies of Mother Earth. We're connected to her, and she'll meet us however it serves us best.

What is Gaia singing to you?

There I stood on a bridge at the Hudson right above the highway and cried. I cried and felt anger and shame. Anger about what we do to the Earth, what we allow to happen to nature, species and the waters of the planet. Shame about knowing all too well that also I was having a part in this. I was angry about how selfish and greedy we'd become. I was really upset. And then I heard an inner voice: *"It won't always be like that. I am cosmic law. The current systems of your world will crumble and fall. Only love will prevail. In the end, only love will last."* Again, energy was rushing through my entire body. The kind of energy I often feel when something sacred has just happened. I knew there would be inevitable ecological changes – personal service was being asked of all of us. Passionate warriors of the Earth, filled with sounding light, driven by their radiant Soul, standing up for truth, creating a new reality born out of faith, advocates for a resurrected, new Earth rising from the ashes like a phoenix.

SoundSoulJournal:

If you'd like, take your journal and sit with your Soul. You might want to sit outside on the ground. Let your entire being be flooded with sounding love. Breathe in your inherent divinity and let go of worries and stress. Breathe in your cosmically sounding essence and breathe out any feeling of depletion or overwhelm. Know that you are loved no matter what; know that you are enough. Take your time and sink into this truth. And when you feel really grounded and connected, ask this question: 'What is my relationship to Earth? How can I contribute to the healing of the planet? Please sing to me Gaia. Sing to me your ancient Song' Just listen. Receive. And when you're filled and nourished to the brim, act.

Soul-centered Activism

WE CAN DO MANY THINGS. We can make a difference and are everything else but helpless. It might start with simple gestures like these: reducing our plastic waste and switching to materials from renewable resources. Having a tote in our bag at all times so we do not ever need to use plastic bags again. Switching to garbage bags that decompose. Examining the clothes we're buying, contributing to a greener planet by wearing sustainable, fair materials. I recently saw a post of a company creating 'paper' plates made out of a special kind of large leaves. Fabulous! Doing our own responsible environmental research. Knowing what's happening to our planet. Reducing CO2 emissions. Taking public transportation whenever possible or switching to a hybrid or electric car. Growing our own vegetables. Cleaning up our neighborhoods. Planting trees. Being in nature regularly, rebuilding our relationship with Mother Earth. Forming circles with like-minded people to discuss the current crises and take action. Raising awareness for the planet and conscious, green living in our communities, neighborhoods, and amongst our friends. Doing so with love but speaking our truth for the environment if necessary.

I would like to introduce you to the work of a spiritual teacher that has influenced me a great deal, Andrew Harvey. Andrew is a modern-day mystic, a scholar, and an environmental activist. He has written numerous books and has a burning passion for our planet. Let me introduce him with his own words about his Institute of Sacred Activism:

"A spirituality that is only private and self-absorbed, one devoid of an authentic political and social consciousness, does little to halt the suicidal juggernaut of history. On the other hand, an activism that is not purified by profound spiritual and psychological self-awareness and rooted in divine truth, wisdom, and compassion will only perpetuate the problem it is trying to solve, however righteous its intentions. When, however, the deepest and most grounded spiritual vision is married to a practical and pragmatic drive to transform all existing political, economic, and social institutions, a holy force - the power of wisdom and love in action - is born. This force I define as Sacred Activism." - *Andrew Harvey, Institute of Sacred Activism*

Andrew initiated great environmental projects such as helping to save the white lions from extinction and much more. His book His book *'Radical Passion: Sacred Love and Wisdom in Action'* addresses the crisis we're facing in a comprehensive, practical way. Let your heart be set on fire for our home, our planet. Let yourself be inspired by those who walk a path of selfless sacred activism, born of and fueled by the Soul.

Weaving a healing tapestry of Sound

Sound is healing. Sound is Life - and Sound will play a major role in building a new heaven-on-Earth-reality on our planet. Our dilemma began with us not hearing Gaia's Song anymore. It started with us underestimating and belittling our fundamental need for nature. It began with us becoming greedy and creating more and more distance between the Earth, her cycles, and us. It all started with us leaving behind our awe for the forces of nature, seeing her solely as something to make a profit from, ignoring that our health desperately depends on communion with nature. We forgot the sacred, ancient Song of the Earth. We built skyscraper after skyscraper, highway after highway, city after city. We pasted and plastered our planet with cement, steel, and plastic and live alienated to the origin we once came from.

The sacred Song of this Earth needs to be heard. Her Sound is not some 'New Age fairytale.' It is real. Gaia is continuously sounding beneath our feet. The turning away from her Song has made us sick and we will only heal if we summon ourselves to listen and live by it again. In 2022, I am launching my *SoundPriestesses Mystery School.* Re-establishing a deep connection to the frequency of our planet – *to the trees, the rocks, the stones, the animal kingdom, the forests, the rivers, and oceans – to Gaia itself* will be a major focus. Learning how to first hear one's own and then Gaia's sacred Song - *and share it* - learning how to pass on the wisdom of her messages will be essential in the healing and transformation of our planet.

The dualistic, linear, patriarchally influenced mind manufactured a spirituality suggesting to leave the body behind to 'climb' higher and higher states of consciousness, escaping the physical and life on Earth. The path of the Soul though is not linearly ascending, out of the body, away from the physical. Divine sounding Source flows through all there is – into all directions and dimensions – and that includes our bodies as well as our planet. The sounding, cosmic veins of life, blazing their way through Mother Earth, want to reach us, flood our beings, and transform our lives. A true spiritual path *is not an upward movement – nor is it a downward movement – it pulls us in;* into sounding Source within, into the dimensions of Soul. What our world needs desperately is an *embodied* form of spirituality – fully and wholly grounded in this life right now, right here on Earth, radiating sounding light from within throughout the physical, manifesting our infinite essence by the kind of lives we live on this planet.

We're called indeed to *weave a sounding tapestry of healing* in cooperation with Earth. Many can feel her call. Many can sense a pull towards her ancient Song. It calls us to return to her. It urges us to honor this terrestrial, ancient home, becoming sounding vessels of embodied grace, transforming ourselves and the planet, helping it shift into divine dimensions once more. .

Tenth Chapter: Practical Service

Manifesting your Divine Vibration

"Hide not your Talents, they for Use were made. What's a Sun-Dial in the shade?" -Benjamin Franklin

SERVICE IS WHAT IS NEEDED. Practical service from the Soul. Service flowing from the Divine Frequency you carry. Service that is Earth-bound. Yes, Earth-bound. Service that manifests your spiritual glory into the physical. Service that will help humanity transition into their sacred vibration again. Service that is golden. Golden because of the Heart-of-Gold that is birthing it. Service that breaks down boundaries of separation and hate. Service that leaves behind physical, tangible results. Results that everyone can see, taste, hear, smell and feel. Results of Gold. Results of the abundance and prosperity of your Soul's vibration.

'What is my service?', you might ask.

Quicken the process of finding your answer by asking yourself: *"What do I most love in this life?", "What could I do for hours and hours without getting tired?", "What fills my heart with joy and a feeling of overflowing gratitude?", "What touches me so deeply that it makes me cry?"*

Ponder on these questions. Take time for reflection, for contemplation. Put yourself in a state of wonder about these questions, like a curious child.

The answers to these questions contain the divine vibration of your Soul – your highest potential. This divine potential has not been given to you to be hidden. It has been given to you to shine like a torch in the night, illuminating many people's way.

The answers to these questions hold a key to what the practical service looks like that you are called to bring to the Earth.

Service that blesses generations. Service that leaves something behind that is far bigger than you. Service that is like a never-ending well, refilling, and refilling you with overflowing joy every time you share.

The answers to these questions want to be reflected in the type of work you do. And if they don't, consider changing careers.

It is time to plug yourself out of draining jobs you hate and instead let the divine potential of your Soul take the lead and create a new reality.

"FEAR NOT, FOR I AM CALLING YOU."

SoundSoulJournal

What do I most love in this life?

What could I do for hours and hours without getting tired?

What fills my heart with joy and a feeling of overflowing gratitude? What touches me so deeply that it makes me cry?

SoulGifts

Your *SoulGifts*, holding the key to your practical Service, are the particular notes making *your* Soul's Song unique. Your SoulGifts are deeply interconnected with why you are here on this planet. You're one of a kind, like a snowflake. There are ways in how you can contribute to the Whole like no other can. Let's peel off some more layers around the practical Service your Soul is calling you to engage with by diving deeper into your unique gifts. The following practice might help you with this:

Take a moment in silence and take a deep breath. Just feel your entire being, your body, your emotions, your heart. Breathe into the base of your spine, feel it tilting into an upright position. Feel your feet on the ground, your sit bones on the chair or floor. Feel your arms hanging freely. Breathe into your heart. Feel your chest rising and falling. Feel your heart getting lighter. Breathe in sounding grace, inherent in your Soul. Relax the space between your eyebrows and become aware of the sounding, liquid golden light entering your body, circulating inside of you, and streaming from you into the world. When you feel grounded, relaxed, and present, ask yourself the following questions:

What am I voraciously passionate about? What fills me with so much excitement that I could talk about it nonstop? What am I really good at? What are my unique Soul gifts?

Some of my deepest passions and SoulGifts are related to music, sound, and voice. I have many interests but Sound and the Divine always surpassed them all. For me, it wasn't a choice to become a musician – I *had* to. In my early twenties, I felt an inner urge to study classical piano and practiced like crazy to get accepted in one of Europe's best schools for music – the Mozarteum in Salzburg to study with Cordelia Hoefer-Teutsch, my piano professor that I mentioned before. And I did. I already told you how I then went from being a piano graduate to becoming an opera singer. This might have sounded like a quick and easy shift but it was one of the most challenging professional and personal transitions I ever committed to. The one thing I knew for sure was I had to become a singer. *I had to sing*. It was like a life-enhancing drug. I was pulled towards singing so strongly - it made me feel so good, so alive - it was inescapable. I practiced and practiced to develop my voice - had my first successes, and as a byproduct got to know myself really well. And then, my Soul took me into a deep dive of discovering that there was a *Sound within; a Sound longing to be expressed* - a Sound that me, the musician, wasn't actually 'producing' - but that was already intrinsically and eternally part of who I am. This perception changed my life entirely.

.

The Kali-Process

HAD YOU ASKED ME a few years ago what my biggest professional goal is, I would have said: *'to become a successful internationally known opera singer.'* That is what I wanted with all of my heart, that is what I was working for. Singing made (and makes) me feel vibrant, radiant, and connected to the core of who I am. I took (and take) countless, pricey voice lessons with some of the best opera teachers in the world. After some years of concentrated dedication in which my voice began to grow, I started to have some successes. I sang in New York City, Boston, Charlotte, Grand Rapids, Seattle, Louisville, and several other places all over the United States.

After some pretty busy opera seasons, my career suddenly slowed down. Out of the blue, I had fewer contracts - and then came a season 2018/19 *(as performers we think in seasons, starting after the summer break until the next)* where I had no contracts at all! I tried to stay calm, singing audition after audition. *No one hired me*. I didn't sing worse than in the time of my successes, rather better - and still, I didn't get hired and I started to freak out. What was going on? Was I not on track anymore? Somewhere deep inside though, there was a knowing of all being in divine order. I couldn't fully grasp what was going on, but I started to get the feeling that there was a deeper meaning behind it all. Little did I know that the Divine was preparing me for a world crisis no one quite expected at that time.

Two years before my operatic regression, I had started a humble online platform for Sound Meditations. I had begun to record personal, intuitive Sound Meditations, touching many people's lives. I knew deep down in myself that I had to expand this work. I knew I was meant to create something bigger than having some kind of a basic website, recording personal Sound Meditations once in a while. There was part of me that knew I had to share what I knew about the mystery of Sound and its sacred, ancient laws, and teach it.

I knew my opera life was in the hands of the Divine, asking me to trust. I began to explore my voice in different ways and discovered new aspects of how one can find healing and personal empowerment through working with the voice. I was super inspired to help others connect with the Song of *their* Soul, thereby heal, and create a glorious life in alignment with their divine vibration.

Once I surrendered to an apparent, yet invisible divine plan, a flood of creative ideas and inspiration began to vividly flow into my life. I often didn't know where to start and how to handle all the impulses coming through. A vast dam had been opened. I could see how the Divine was transitioning me into new, untouched professional territory.

My Soul has led me to create all kinds of sounding projects. One of them, you are holding in your hands right now. If 1:1 or group sessions, Sound and its connection to God is the predominant motor of every aspect of my business. My sounding calling seems to be continuously expanding; you can find out more on *www.soundingsouls.com*.

Two elements of my business I wanna highlight though. First, In 2022, the *SoundPriestess Mystery School* is being launched for the first time, bringing together and training the Daughters of New Earth who are called to work with sacred Sound and become sounding channels of divine transformation. This movement is kickstarted with a Bootcamp of pioneering ladies in May 2022, setting foundations for the School. We still have open spaces - and if you're reading this after May 15th 2022, you can join the Mystery School later on.

Second, in March 2022, I started working with the frequencies of physical Gold and Silver out of an intuitive guidance I received, and am creating an abundant business around it (more about that in just a moment). My vision is to become so abundant that I can bring forth art centers and entire high quality sacred art-eco-sound-spaces in geodesic domes, based on organic living in harmony with Mother Gaia, free from the medical tyranny of dark powers.

My Soul took me on a professional path I didn't quite expect. I'm deeply humbled to be doing what I do today; ever more deeply exploring the connection of Sound and Soul and teaching what I've learned. It fills my heart with joy every day of my life. It is my practical service.

As my story might show, it can be challenging to surrender our ideas to a higher plan. I call the professional expansion I was going through *the Kali-process*. Kali is an archetype of the Divine Feminine - known as the Goddess of death, transformation, and resurrection, rising from the ashes like the phoenix. Something inside me had to *'die,'* like a *Phoenix* and had to be transformed so a deeper version of my calling could be born. My inner Kali had to do her purifying magic, alchemizing and healing my being through her divine fires to a deeper level of remembering the Song of my Soul. Performing and practicing singing is still part of my life, but my approach to Sound, my motivations, and my understanding of it have shifted majorly.

You see, it is a *journey*. And wherever you are right now is the perfect place to grow deeper into your truth. This chapter is here to help you become aware of how you are called to be of practical service, manifesting your divine vibration in Earth-bound ways, and align your life accordingly. This chapter is about igniting a flame in your heart and encouraging you to follow the gentle voice inside that's maybe pointing in a different direction than what you had in mind. Maybe you are experiencing a similar *Kali-transformation-process* as I did. If you do, congratulations, you are right on track. Maybe you have an inner *'entrepreneur'* slumbering inside of you and you feel you are meant to build *your* version of a Soul-centered business. Then this next section is for you.

Blossoming Business

Mother Earth is one of the greatest teachers we have when it comes to sustainably growing anything. She is the mentor of mentors, the ancient Wise One. When I was confused about strategies I saw other so-called 'spiritual coaches' apply that felt inauthentic and draining to me, *She* called me to spend time with her to receive and simply listen. I did. *I do*. I'm spending time with her daily. Her trees are a source of inspiration to me; they are tall, loving, wise teachers whose wisdom we can plug into. By consciously watching the organic processes of nature we learn so much. If we listen regularly to the wisdom of Mother Earth, our psychic antennas get sharper and sharper, and then it is only a question of trusting and integrating what we hear.

Rooted in the time I spend in nature's classroom, I created my SoulBusiness. Based on the organic laws of Mother Gaia, my work thrives. She taught me fundamental principles. Principles that make the trees grow and the flowers blossom. Some of these principles I'm gonna share with you now.

'If nothing's inside, nothing can grow out of it'

Does nature throw *empty shells* on the ground in the hope they'd magically turn into trees? Of course not! Tree seeds contain all the data needed for growing into a small sapling, slowly but surely evolving into a teenage tree, an adolescent tree, until a mature, strong tree further expands in front of our eyes. The little seed contains it all and is part of the whole.

Nothing can truly grow without being interconnected and filled with Source. Nothing. We would all agree on how preposterous it is to think a plant could grow out of an empty shell. And yet, when it comes to creating businesses, to advertising and self-promotion via social media, we seem to forget this truth. We are contaminated by the strategies of modern economy; all being about quantity, followers, selling numbers, quick profit, tricking people into buying our 'products' with promising slogans, and forgetting nature's simplest law: *'If nothing's inside, nothing can grow out of it.'*

We can only truly offer to others what we have embodied, what we have gained a certain maturity in. What's needed is a deep anchoring in our Soul, committed to facing our own fears, shadows, and projections. No one can build a sustainable, successful, life-bringing business, project, or organization without dedication and hard work, fed by the infinite reality within. Remember the seasons? There is the heat of summer and the introspection of winter. There are natural cycles in place to support the process of maturation. Trust that the seeds and fruits you're meant to share will evolve organically, filled with authentic transformational power.

'It takes time'

A tree never worries about how he will grow into a big, strong tree. He doesn't even think about growing at all. He simply is plugged into the natural cycles, organically participating in the laws of Mother Earth - and without knowing, he grows. If we would only realize that building a relationship to the inner Sound of our Soul and stepping into our callings are feeding into each other. Look at any plant. The apple doesn't magically appear at a tree's branch overnight. It is slowly being formed, undergoing many stages from a tender blossom to a mini fruit, before becoming a sweet ripe apple. Isn't it such a gift that we can allow things to grow *organically*? Is it not so wonderful that the Soul doesn't want us to be 'non-stop creators', exploiting our resources? Isn't it so soothing to allow our businesses, projects, organizations, or creative endeavors to undergo natural cycles - cycles of reflection, planning, blossoming, growing, harvesting, *and* resting?

We need to water our vision, we need to expose the saplings to the sun. And sometimes we need to aerate the soil to stay receptive. Once in a while, we have to weed the garden, meaning, we need to go deep into ourselves and examine what it is we are growing and course-correct if necessary. There is no shame in this - it's all part of the process. But it *takes time* to attend to these important elements of growth.

Building a business of any kind is a lot of work - and you will need perseverance and stamina *and holy days of rest* in between if what you want to create is supposed to be sustainable. Your body will signal to you what you need and I encourage you to follow its advice. No matter how excited you might be about your project, it is physically, emotionally, and spiritually impossible to create non-stop. Your vision will die within months if you don't balance intense phases of working with *self-care and rest,* letting it take the time it needs.

'The Bridge'

I love the symbolism of a bridge. It connects. It brings people from one reality to another, bridging invincible waters or valleys. Offering our Soul gifts to the world can be compared to building a bridge - helping people to expand into their very own Soul reality. How we build that bridge, how we maintain it, how we treat people who cross over it will decide on whether our endeavor will succeed or not. Are we building with materials of integrity? Are we following an inner compass of authenticity? Are we responsible in engineering, making sure our bridge won't collapse?

Once people start crossing our bridge, how do we treat them? Do we bring them a glass of water, are we lovingly encouraging them to keep on walking and cross over to the other side? Are we permitting them to rest if necessary? Are we detached enough to be okay with people feeling our bridge isn't the right fit for them, letting them go with a blessing in our hearts?

'Know the size of thy house'

The question of how many people our business or project can 'host' yet is quite essential. If we long our professional lives to thrive and be life-promoting, we have to be aware of not wanting to grow too big too fast. In all seriousness, *know the size of thy house.* Know the capacity and stability of your interior life. How much at home are you in yourself? How much are you grounded in what's true *for you*? How easy is it for you to detect your own projections? Are you able to radiate your inner sounding grace without compromising your overall well-being? Can you responsibly hold space for ten, twenty, fifty, a hundred people? Please don't underestimate the energy and stamina it takes to invite people to cross your bridge. *You are being the bridge yourself* - called to sing the Song of your Soul, inviting many to step into the sounding, liberating essence of their nature.

Golden Abundance

Gold. Gold. Gold. Feeling the vibration of this word. Sensing it. Like you would sense the smell of a beautiful flower. Gold is a divine substance. Gold is divine frequency. Gold is a physical expression of the vibration of God. Gold is solidified sunlight; sunlight of the central sun, carrying the Song of the Mother. Meditate on it. Use it as a Mantra. *Gold. Gold. Gold.* Sound the word *Gold.* Breathe in Gold. Inhale golden substance through the top of your head into your pineal gland, expanding into a golden sun at the center of your brain with your exhale. Breathe Gold into every organ of your body. Become Gold. Become Gold in your perceptions. Become Gold in your heart. Become Gold in your mind. BE GOLD.

Many of us are called to *have* physical Gold and live in its vibration. Gold carries divine vibration. Gold is SoundMoney. Money that's actual money. Money that's real. Gold is SoundMoney. Gold as well as Silver. Imagine yourself living in a palace of gold. In a place where everything is made of gold. The bathtub, the tables, the chairs, and everything else. It will help your subconscious to attract Gold and live in its divine vibration of pure abundance in everything you do. Gold attracts Gold. You might want to have some at your home. Because you are a child of God.

You can breathe in Gold into everything you do. Every creative project. Every business idea. Every relationship. Every child you are to bear. Every aspect of live can be filled with the vibration of gold.

Gold is much "older" than many of us think. It does not only exist on our planet but in many places of this universe. And it belongs to the children of God. There is a reason why the manipulating forces have kept away gold and silver and made it almost inaccessible for the average person. Now is the time where the children of DivineSoundingSource are taking back their power and have Gold. Gold and Silver.

About a year ago, I felt a strong urge to dive deeper into Gold and Silver. The universe brought to a membership around Gold and Silver my way that's open for everyone, providing a sound education about Gold and Silver, a safe access to proven precious metals and so much more. I even created an abundant business around it! To learn more, click here, or look for Gold on my website (www.soundingsouls.com).

SoundSoulJournal:

What is your relationship to abundance? What is your relationship to gold & silver?

Eleventh Chapter: The Song of the Aquarian Age

Bestowing Healing upon the Land

"Major waves of healing and transformation will flow to this world through Sound - one of the most effective and holistic tools of transformation."
-Magdalene Gartner

Eleven is a sacred and potent number.It is the second last in the sacred cycle of twelve that we need to look at first. There are twelve months of the year, twelve hours a day, and twelve a night. In Greek mythology, there are twelve main gods, the Zodiac has twelve signs. Jesus supposedly picked twelve apostles, there are the twelve tribes of Israel. In many sacred texts, twelve is a number of completion and harmony. Twelve as a number plays a major role in the division of tones and frequencies in music. In more ancient times, girls and boys were initiated into adulthood at the age of twelve. Eleven as a number thereby stands for being close to the completion of a phase, close to a new cycle to start, close to a major shift.

Without having planned it, this chapter about the Aquarian Song fell onto the eleventh phase of our journey. Now, where is the sign of Aquarius positioned in the zodiac? It is the *eleventh* sign, representing the last *air* sign of the cycle. Aquarius is the water bearer, and since it is an air sign, we could more appropriately say *the light bearer - a mystical healer who bestows light* - live-bringing frequency - *upon the land.* The cosmic cycle we are transitioning into is characterized by this mystic symbolism. It calls humanity to grow up and step into its sacred, full potential. There's no more time for playing small, for getting stuck behind a victim mentality, for projecting our responsibility – us embracing the radiating Song of our Souls and practically bestowing sounding light upon 'the land' has never been more urgent than *now.*

An Aquarian Pioneer

JOSEF WAS THE ELEVENTH SON of Jacob, one of the three patriarchs of Israel whose sons were to form the twelve tribes of the new nation. Josef was born to Rachel, the wife Jacob dearly loved. Jacob had been tricked and forced by his wicked father in law to marry Leah first, Rachel's older sister. Leah now was quite fruitful and bore Jacob many sons. Rachel, instead, was barren. Ten sons had already been born to Jacob when Rachel eventually became pregnant and gave birth to her first son which she named Josef, meaning *'he will add'* or *'God increases'*. Jacob loved him dearly, favoring and spoiling Josef, which caused raging jealousy amongst the older brothers.

Young Josef had a unique gift. He was a dreamer. From an early age, he had dreams with significant meaning that he knew how to interpret. Josef was capable of decoding the dream's message - he understood its symbolic language. When he was still a teenager, Josef had two dreams. In the first one, he saw eleven bundles of crops belonging to his eleven brothers. (Rachel had given birth to one more son, Benjamin, making them twelve brothers in total.) In the dream, all eleven bundles of his brothers were bowing down before Josef's bundle, paying him respect. Josef, still being young and naive, shared the dream with his brothers telling them how their bundles bowed down before his.

Now, we need to understand, the ten older brothers were adult men. Most of them already had families and established livestock - strong men that worked hard every day, managing and multiplying the numerous flocks of their wealthy father Jacob. Here their little spoiled teenage brother Josef comes, telling them his dream. They weren't happy.

Some days after this affair, Josef said to his father: "I had another dream, and this time the sun and moon and eleven stars were bowing down to me." His brothers listened when father Jacob rebuked him and said, "What kind of a dream is this? Do you really think your mother and I and your brothers will actually come and bow down to the ground before you?" Hearing what Josef had dreamt again now infuriated the brothers even more. Old father Jacob though, having experienced divine guidance through dreams when he was a young man, kept the matter in his heart..

The days went by until one day, Jacob summoned Josef to bring refreshments to his brothers who were out in the fields, guarding the flocks in the heat of the day. Poor Josef, dressed in a new garment the father had just given him, unknowingly arrived when his ten brothers seized him, threw him into a deep fountain, and sold him to a passing caravan, consumed by their jealousy. Killed by the wild beasts Josef had been - so they told their devastated father which broke the old man. Josef, however, was brought to Egypt as a slave where he served in the house of Potifar, an Egyptian aristocrat. He was skilled in managing the affairs of the men and soon enough Potifar entrusted Josef with the entire household - he became Potifar's first manager. Everything Josef touched seemed to be blessed and he was highly respected by his master and the other servants.

Now the story goes that Josef was a handsome, well-built young man. His looks sparked the interest of Potifar's wife, who approached him to lay with her. Josef resisted her advances knowing only too well that he wouldn't only lose his job but his life if he slept with the wife of his master. Offended by his refusal, the aristocrat's wife designed an evil plan. She called Josef, approaching him once more while no one else was in the house. Josef ran away, leaving his cloak in her room that she had furiously grabbed. Potifar's wife began to scream, calling for her servants. She claimed Josef had tried to enforce himself on her, running away when she refused. When she told her rakish version of the story to her husband, Potifar was infuriated and threw his Hebrew slave into prison - the prison of the Pharaoh.

Josef wasn't there for long when he gained the favor of the guards, who put him in charge of everything that was happening inside the prison walls. Whatever Josef took in his hands was a success. Even though he was officially an inmate, he was the prison's first manager, trusted by all. One day, two of the Pharaoh's servants - his cupbearer and baker - were thrown into prison. Both of the men had vivid dreams the following night, sharing them with the other prisoners the next morning. Josef listened to their dreams and immediately delivered an interpretation. The cupbearer would be restored into his office in three days, while the baker would be hanged. Both of his interpretations came to pass in the exact way Josef had prophesied.

Two years went by - Josef was still managing the Pharaoh's prison - when the ruler of Egypt unexpectedly suffered from disturbing dreams. He called his advisors and astrologers but no one was able to help him. At this moment, the cupbearer, who was restored into his office as Josef had said, remembered the prison's manager. He told the king about the accuracy of Josef's dream interpretations and immediately the Pharaoh sent for him. In the presence of the court and all assembled royal advisors, the Pharaoh shared his dreams with Josef, who listened carefully and told him what they meant without hesitation. The dreams were of utter importance for the Egyptian empire, pointing to a horrendous famine that would break out and last for seven years. Before the famine, though, would be seven years of utter abundance. If the country prepared itself, the crops were properly managed, stored, so Josef said, Egypt would survive the famine.

In an instant, while standing before one of the world's most powerful leaders at the time, Josef reluctantly interpreted the dreams and proposed a practical, comprehensive plan on how to organize, store, and prepare for the famine. As a response, the Pharaoh appointed Josef to be in charge of the preparations for the famine, set him over the entire country, and named Josef the second man ruling over Egypt. Only the throne itself should separate Josef from the Pharaoh.

And so our teenage boy from a Hebrew tribe of wandering wealthy nomads got to work. Josef thoroughly prepared Egypt in the following seven years that *were* indeed abundant and well needed for the famine to come. His skills and wisdom were praised throughout Egypt. Thanks to Josef the empire had enough supplies when no more crops were growing. Egypt had to eat, its cities equipped with well-organized food storages.

But not only Egypt was affected by the famine, countries close-by were too. And so it happened that old Jacob and his entire stock and family suffered severely. Rumors had spread that Egypt would have storages full of grain and so Jacob entrusted his ten oldest sons to go to Egypt and buy food for the starving family. Packed with sacks of gold, they took off for the foreign land. Exhausted they arrived and were not exactly met with hospitality. Because the Hebrews were mistrusted strangers in Egypt who could have been spies, the ten men were brought to the palace of the Pharaoh's right hand to speak for themselves, not recognizing their brother in the fine garments of his royal Egyptian outfit. *They bowed down to the earth*, telling the Egyptian ruler that their old father Jacob had sent them to buy food. Josef didn't believe what he was seeing. He had to hide his face, leave the room, and cry behind the scenes. It was his brothers! There they stood, his own brothers who had thrown him into a well and sold him as a slave. His heart was overwhelmed. It was filled with compassion for his family. What was to do next?

Josef went back to his brothers and said, "How is your old father?" Now, Josef dearly loved his younger brother Benjamin, the only other child of Rachel, his mother. "Is that your entire family or is there another brother of yours?" And they told him about their youngest brother Benjamin and how the father had kept him home because he already lost one son and didn't want to lose his youngest too. Josef said to them: "You must be spies. How can I know that I can trust you? I shall only know that you are speaking the truth if you go back home, and bring back your youngest brother Benjamin. I shall keep one of you here until the day of your return. Do not dare to appear before my eyes again without your youngest brother." And so they traveled back home - their donkeys packed with sacks of grain while their brother Simeon was kept in Egyptian custody.

Old Jacob wasn't happy when they arrived back home. Give away his youngest son, after he had already lost Josef? Letting Benjamin go with his nine remaining sons who just came back from Egypt without Simeon? But the famine was severe and forced the large family to do as the foreign ruler of Egypt had commanded. If they wanted to survive, they had to go back, take Benjamin with them, and buy more food.

Josef got informed about his brothers' second arrival and had a big meal prepared - all to their confusion. After that, he had their sacks filled with grain, smuggled a silver cup in Benjamin's sack, and told them to leave. A few hours after their departure, Josef sent after them, having his soldiers open the sacks of the men, and taking them back to Josef since they obviously were thieves and had 'stolen' a precious silver cup. The brothers were terrified because of all the people, the cup had been found in *Benjamin's* sack of grain, the youngest brother their father was most worried about. Josef, well understanding what they said to each other in their mother tongue sensed their fear and deep regret. There was remorse in their hearts for having sold their brother Josef. They believed the famine and the difficulties with this Egyptian ruler were brought upon them as a punishment from God.

The hour had come. Josef commanded all servants to leave the room, took off his Egyptian clothes, and spoke to them: "I am your brother, Joseph, whom you sold as a slave. Don't be afraid because you sold me here, because *God sent me here before you to preserve life.* The famine has been in the land for two years but there are yet five years in which there will be neither plowing nor harvest. God sent me before you to preserve your tribe on earth, and to keep alive your children. *So it was not you who sent me here, but God.* He has made me a father to Pharaoh, lord of all his house and ruler over all the land of Egypt. Hurry and go up to my father and say to him, 'Thus says your son Joseph, God has made me lord of all Egypt. Come down to me; do not tarry. You shall dwell in the land of Goshen, and you shall be near me, you and your children and your children's children, and your flocks, your herds, and all that you have. '(Genesis 45)."

Can you imagine their faces?

~~~

I TOLD YOU THE STORY OF JOSEPH because there is so much to learn from it. Josef's life is the perfect aquarian example. He had a calling not only to save the entire nation of Egypt but also to preserve the life of his own family out of which emerged the nation of Israel. *He was sent to Egypt for a divine purpose.*

Josef could have gotten stuck in bitterness. Oh yes, he could have. He could have become angry for having to endure all this pain, for losing his family, and for not being with his beloved father and mother anymore. But Josef had enough trust in the Divine that he managed to stay open to whatever difficulty life threw at him. For many years, he endured being a slave, sold by his own brothers because of their envy. He served a master in a culture foreign to him but was able to adapt and excel in anything he did. Then he was betrayed *again*, mistreated, and thrown into prison for something he didn't do. Another moment in which Josef could have said: 'Enough already! I'm not doing anything wrong and again and again, I am
~~~

being punished, betrayed, and humiliated.' But Josef was living in another dimension. He didn't allow outer humiliation to determine his inner dignity. He knew his life was in the hands of the Divine. He knew if he trusted and was faithful in whatever he would do - if he made use of the gifts of his Soul - there would be flow, purpose, and life. And so it was. The universe must have looked at Josef, saying: "Yes! He's ready. He has the backbone for the task we'd like him to fulfill. He stays strong and true to his Soul no matter what. He's our guy!"

Do you see how *betrayal* played a major role in the path of Josef living up to his highest potential? He would probably never have ended up in Egypt without his brothers selling him. He would have never gotten to the chambers of the Pharaoh, interpreting his dreams, had he not been thrown into the king's prison, meeting the cupbearer of the ruler of Egypt who later remembered Josef's talent. Josef had to spend many years in Egypt, learn the language, and adapt to Egyptian culture long before he was ready to become the second ruler in the empire. If you had asked him at age seventeen if this would be a description of his dream life - had he known all the details his path would entail, he would probably have said: *"No, thank you. Not doing that. Send someone else and leave me alone."* In the process of his challenging life, however, Josef grew the inner muscles of perseverance and devotion to his Soul. Despite many trials, he kept his heart open and trusted the Divine. Wherever he was, he served others with his gifts and surrendered to a plan bigger than what he possibly could have imagined.

Where in your life do *you* feel betrayed? Is it possible that a divine intelligence orchestrated this betrayal for a reason much bigger than you? So you could grow and mature into your potential? Is it possible that there is a higher force behind your life, bringing together the necessary pieces of a puzzle whose size you do not know yet? How do you deal with betrayal in your life? Are you able to keep your heart open, trust, and improvise if life wasn't playing out the way you wanted? How anchored are we in the truth of our Soul, knowing in any situation that our life is in the hands of God - *not of men*?

SoundSoulJournal

In the reflection section of this book is room to dive into these questions.

Crisis as Catalyst

IN THE MIDST OF BETRAYAL, Josef trusted his Soul and simply did what he was good at - he followed *his Soul's gifts, managed, oversaw,* improving his environment for the good of all, and he *interpreted dreams*. That was it. Did he know when he sat in prison that he would become the second ruler over the empire of Egypt, saving an entire nation from starvation? He probably had *no idea*! What he *did* know was that his life was divinely orchestrated, no matter what his outer circumstances looked like. What he *did* know was how to trust and be faithful to his Soul, letting life flow right through him, rather than resisting it. What he knew was how to forgive and let go of bitterness.

And herein lies a divine key: When it comes to our divine calling, we often have to go through painful circumstances in order to get to where we're meant to be to serve the whole. If we knew beforehand about the betrayals on our way that function as catalyzers to bring forth in us the stamina and qualities we need to fill our calling, we wouldn't set one step in front of the door. We would remain in our four walls, on the couch watching TV (or a different monotone comfort zone), wondering why life is so boring.

Does following our calling *always* hurt? Does it *always* lead through painful experiences? I don't think so - but quite honestly, it seems that betrayal and painful experiences often function as a means of transportation to whatever we came to this planet for. Crisis and difficult experiences seem to be transforming by default. *How* they change us is up to us. If we learn to zoom out of any challenging experience into the perspective of an eagle, accepting that there are things we do not understand, hanging uncompromisingly onto our

Soul in the midst of the storm, grace can flow into our lives in unexpected ways.

What are you pouring on the Earth?

The eleventh phase of our journey is about our relationship to the world. It is about our *personal Aquarius calling* - it is about examining what *we* are pouring upon the Earth. Literally and symbolically. We can either generate healing and goodness or pollute and contaminate our surroundings. There is pollution of various kinds. We have environmental pollution, but also psychic, energetic, and also spiritual pollution. Without discernment and staying rooted in our connection to the Divine every day, we easily get toxified by thoughtforms and systems having nothing in common with the inner Sound of the Soul. Like never before, we need mystical healers that have the courage to speak up, create innovative new ways, inspire others to go inward first and heal, and then press ahead with the transformation gearing us into our divine potential.

Bestowing sounding Healing

Our world is aching - it is chronically ill. *We need to 'sound' ourselves back into remembering our divine nature.* We need to deeply anchor ourselves in truth again, and that truth needs to be felt by our whole being, not just our minds. Healing cannot be taught like a dogma. It needs to be experienced. I believe 'sounding' is one of the major ways we can heal as a collective because it unifies so many parts of who we are: the physical-biochemical, the emotional, the mental, the psychic, the energetic, the etheric, and the spiritual. Self-Sounding is a direct path to our divine *sounding* essence. *If we are Sound, sounding will bring us back home.* rld is aching - it is chronically ill. We need to 'sound' ourselves back into remembering our divine nature. We need to deeply anchor ourselves in truth again, and that truth needs to be felt by our whole being, not just our minds. Healing cannot be taught like a dogma. It needs to be holistically experienced. I believe 'sounding' is one of the major ways how we can heal as a collective because it unifies so many parts of who we are: the physical-biochemical, the emotional, the mental, the psychic, the energetic, and the spiritual. Self-Sounding is a direct path to our divine sounding essence. If we are Sound, sounding will bring us back home.

We need Songs of Life that penetrate our beings, creating new pathways in our brains – pathways of light and transformation. Just as in the aboriginal creation myth the Earth was sung into existence, we need to *birth our world again and sing it back into its divine essence.*

The Divine is fully present in every cell of our bodies and is calling upon our ability to *sound* for the sake of healing. We're called to come together and sing healing into our lives and communities. Sounding Source is bestowing healing on circles of SoundingSouls so they in return can become transmitters of grace wherever they are. *SoundingVeins* is a virtual and in-person space I felt called to create a little while ago. When I got clearer on the vision for this endeavor, I heard that this *is a space for Earthians to sing again.* If humans only came back to their birthright to sing and sound.... So, we come together and sound. We sound healing into our personal lives and into the collective. Into our creative projects and visions. Into whatever needs a holy-moly infusion of divine frequency.

The mystic symbolism of Aquarius

THE MORE I REFLECTED on the symbolism of the Aquarius, bearing light-filled energy and pouring healing upon the Earth, the more I realized the mystic truth hidden in it. First, let's look at the target – *upon the land, upon the Earth.* The healing waters are being poured onto the physical, embodied life here on this planet, right now, right here.

The focus of the true mystic healer of the Aquarian Age doesn't lie in reaching higher and higher states of consciousness, *'freeing himself'* of this world - as so many spiritual traditions teach and taught us, degrading the physical life here on earth to second or third class. The true aquarian mystic is fully engaged with the raw and sometimes bewildering life down here on this planet. That's his secret. Nothing is bewildering to him. He sees the sacred in all there is. In the midst of all that life brings, may it be overflowing joy, excruciating pain, blissful ecstasy, or devastating betrayal, he stays open to the Divine and becomes a channel of grace, bestowing healing upon his brothers and sisters, upon his communities, upon the world. He lets himself be cleansed by divine-sounding light first and then pours *himself* unto the earth for this is his calling.

The truth is, we always are channels if we are aware of it or not. Through our lives, we are pouring ourselves upon the 'land' - our loved ones, friends, colleagues, neighbors, and communities. Whatever we are filled with overflows to the outside. There is a reason why we took so much time in the first part of this book to set foundations, to go deep and dive into our personal shadows, into our repressed emotions and underlying patterns. *The essence we are pouring upon the Earth will only carry healing to the extent that we worked through our own shadow.* And I need to add that the shadow isn't anything bad – it is simply an unconscious part of ourselves. The shadow is neither something we can mentalize away by trying to be positive at all times. The moment we're under pressure, our shadow with its unconscious patterns appears and takes over– and then we're not pouring healing but toxic sewage.

When I wrote this chapter, I asked myself the question, "Where is the healing Song of the Aquarian from? Where did he learn to sing and pour it upon the land? Where does he fill himself with healing Sound?" *He went into the deep waters of the realm of his Soul.* That's where the abundant well is hidden. And so, entering the aquarian age, we are *all* called to live in deep oceanic Soul reality, letting the

Song of our Soul guide us in ever deeper healing and transformation – and at the same time fully engage with life right here, right now. *We are called to live in both dimensions simultaneously.* Therein lies no contradiction. Both realities are overlapping in eternal cosmic expansion and creation. When we feel empty, we simply go back into the waters, back into the chambers of our Soul. Back into the endlessness of the Divine Sound of Source, ready to fill us once again.

We are not meant to flee this life. We are here to live it. We are not meant to run away from our physical experience, being afraid of engaging with life! We are meant to live life to the fullest, experience every nuance of it, from making love to eating delicious food to feeling vibrant and alive in our sacred body temples, creating the life of our wildest dreams – and recognize how the divine Song sounds in every breath we take.

The Song of our Soul plugged into Sounding Source is like a sacred spiral. It pulls us *in*. It pulls us into the reality of our Soul, into the reality of the Divine. Once we've arrived in that reality, soaked by light and empowered through recognizing our true, eternal nature, our Soul redirects us to emerge from the waters and pour our sounding Soul-essence upon the land. Many of us believe that a spiritual path means climbing the ladder of consciousness, out of the body and *upwards* into cosmic awareness. I believe this understanding is a result of patriarchal thinking, based on the belief that growth means *'upwards,' 'bigger,' 'higher,' 'more.'* I believe a spirituality promoting such linearity is contaminated by the psychic virus of our days telling us unless we endlessly grow upwards, ignoring the fact that our roots are getting thinner and thinner, we are worthless. A misleading concept of growth completely disassociated from the laws of nature. Think for a second about how the universe is expanding. For some reason, we associate growth only with growing upwards, growing into height while this is not at all how nature is expanding and growing. Nature grows and expands into all directions, into all dimensions. Any tree is proof of that. The universe is expanding into all directions, *multi-dimensional*, like a huge expanding spherical ball.

Why would we have been sent here, why would our Soul have agreed to incarnate into this physical life if the only goal was to escape? The healing waves of the Divine Song are flowing like veins right through the Earth, they are sounding throughout our planet and our bodies. Our life here on Earth isn't an obstacle on our journey to the Divine. At this moment, we are meant to be *here*. Our aching world needs us to be fully present in the now, fully present in the life we have been given. It needs modern-day mystics that know how to fill themselves with divine Sound, build inner muscles of integrity, speaking up for truth, and, therefore, pouring and filling themselves in a mode of a continuous sacred cycle. We need SoundingSouls being at home in multiple dimensions simultaneously, creating Heaven on Earth. We need aquarian healers anchored in their Souls to such an extent that nothing in the world, neither crisis nor betrayal, neither threats nor humiliation, neither global plandemics nor manipulating, evil forces could ever hold them back from following the truth of their mystic calling.

Sounding Fields of Grace leading to Practical Service

I ALREADY MENTIONED MY FRIENDS AT THE SIKH TEMPLE in NYC, Queens, and how they are singing while cooking, sounding heartwarming blessings into the food they serve to hundreds of people every single day. These Sikhs are generating fields of healing and grace, fields of compassion, and a real sense of community that soothes my entire being every time I go there. It is not just their food. It is the light in their eyes, it is the kindness with which they speak. Their entire tradition is based on *Sound* - they're *singing* perpetually. The Sikhs believe in a book of wisdom gathered by their Gurus. They don't preach from the book in their get-togethers, nor have I heard them speak all that much about it - *they sing it*. Their services consist of sounding - musicians who sing love songs to the Divine, engaging the entire congregation. My mind does not understand much of the words - but my Soul does - their songs are floating love, tangible compassion

When I am at their temple, standing amongst many hundred singing Sikhs, I feel like I am standing in a huge field of pulsing grace. It feels like I am surrounded by atmospheric, wholesome thick ether. I look at their lit-up faces. Young and old gathered together - all singing light into each other's beings. They sing from their belly, they don't sing because they have to; they don't sing solely from their minds - they sing because *sounding* for them is a deep expression of their Soul, needing to be channeled into the physical. It sounds as if they are *'being sung',* sung by myriads of divine light beings bridging the seen and unseen worlds – and yet – that's not all they do. These Sikhs are *hands-on*, hard working people, serving their community with a level of dedication and commitment you don't see very often. They have very practical ways of service, e.g., feeding thousands of Souls every day. And that brings me to my last point of this chapter.

"I am not interested in the Etheric"

A little while ago I heard in my spirit while being in a meditative space, "I am not interested in the Etheric. I am interested in the Physical. What do you most desire to create? What is there, deep down in the treasure land of your heart that you dream of and long to manifest?"

First, I was stunned. "You are not interested in the Etheric?" And then an inner dialogue started. A dialogue in which I was told that it wasn't about the Etheric, it wasn't about having experiences in the spiritual realms. At least, that was only half of the deal. It was about bringing the glory of our divine vibration to Earth. In tangible, physical forms, for all to see. That means work. That means getting our hands dirty. That means dedication, persistence and commitment to birthing into the world that which we are called to birth.

For me, I sound about everything in my life. I go into sound when I need instructions of how to go about the visions I am called to manifest. I go into sound when I create a new online course, or when I am about to launch an event. I go into sounding about how to build my business around Gold and Silver, and when it comes to what to teach in the SoundPriestess Mystery School. I go into sounding about everything I do.

Here's the deal: Sounding is a gateway connecting to your Soul. You receive the guidance and strategies on how to manifest what you desire to bring to this world. And then you do it. Simple. Not necessarily easy, but simple.

What are you called to birth? What is your aquarian calling? The systems of this world are not based on sacred vibration. We need to restructure and rebuild everything we do as the collective human community. How to educate our children in a sacred way, how to live in harmony with Mother Earth, how to do business in an alignment with our Soul, how to do medicine, how to live in unity consciousness and universal laws, how to take care of our elders, how to live in community, how to have new, sustainable architectural structures that honor life, how to do therapy, how to do finances, how to have sacred relationships, how to....... fill in the blank. It's not enough to sit down and meditate, dance or go to a New Earth festival. What are you called to bring to the physical? What is your aquarian calling?

This is an invitation to live from the realm of your Soul, and then BIRTH into the physical that divine vibration that you are. Get your hands dirty. Work. Give it your best shot! Be bold. Dream big. No change was ever created by those sitting around waiting for better times. As Jesus would say to the lame man: "Get up your bed and walk!" This is the true meaning of being in but not of the world, this is the true meaning of creating Heaven on Earth.

Twelfth Chapter: The Song of the Mother

Surrendering to the Sounding Spiral of the Divine Feminine

"From the ashes, a fire shall be woken, a light from the shadows shall spring."
-J.R.R. Tolkien

The Song of the Mother is real. There is nothing more soothing than her Song. The enveloping, all-encompassing veil of velvet placed around your shoulders, the buzzing vibration filling your entire being like a ringing bell, the gentle voice inside calling you home is unfathomable.

A lady who is part of the SoundPriestess Movement recently shared with the group after we did some serious sounding, *"I feel like a bell. My whole body feels like a huge bell!"* – that is what the Song of the Mother does. It enlivens. It heals. It uplifts. It nourishes. It extends itself through us. It changes the atmosphere all around us. It calls her children home. I believe we're meant to feel like vibrating bells all the time!

Try this with me: Here's a Mantra of the Mother. A Mantra of Shakti. Chant it with me and let's see how you feel. The *Shakti Mantra* in ancient Sanskrit calls upon *'the Great Goddess of the Universe'*. Shakti is an archetype of the Divine Feminine and creative power. She is present in every part of the energetic web of the universe, rushing through the veins of our bodies and the Earth beneath our feet, breathing life into every planet and star in the galaxies, being omnipresent and manifest in all there is. Shakti is considered the Great Goddess of Source. If you open up to her, your life will never be the same. She is the Goddess of Creation. The universe is her womb from which we all originated. Whoever feels her all-encompassing embrace will never want to be anywhere else than inside her sounding spiral of universal, unconditional love. Chant this mantra if you long to encounter her. She will show up if you do. In her, we live and have our being. Chant the mantra in your own way, or join me in the recording you find below in your Virtual Library.

So far, we haven't talked about the word *'remember.'* Interestingly, it contains the word *'member.'* Re-member-ing, therefore, means to bring something back into its rightful membership. Re-***member***-ing the Song of our Soul; decoding our divine vibration really means that we see ourselves as members of the Cosmic Whole - of the Cosmic Song. We are re-*member*-ing ourselves by realizing that we have been *members* of the Divine Symphony *all along*.

Adi Shakti Adi Shakti Adi Shakti, Namo Namo
Sarab Shakti Sarab Shakti Sarab Shakti, Namo Namo
Pritam Bhagvati Pritam Bhagavati Pritam Bhagavati, Namo Namo
Kundalini Mata Shakti Mata Shakti, Namo Namo

Here is a rough translation:

I bow (or call upon) to the Primal Power within.

I bow to the all-encompassing Power and Energy.
I bow to that through which Goddess creates.
I bow to the creative power of the kundalini, the Divine Mother Power.

VIRTUAL LIBRARY:

Adi Shakti ~ A Sound Meditation of the Divine Feminine

There are many ways to encounter the Song of the Mother. *"Why"*, you might say. *"Why do I need the Mother? Which Mother? I thought this is about the Song of my Soul!"* What if the Song of the Mother was the Song of your Soul? What if you would not even exist without her Song running through your veins? What if there was such a craving for the Divine Feminine in our age; such a craving for the nourishment and healing of the Mother that she decided to vibrate in your Soul even stronger at this time? What if what you're longing for the most - *unconditional love* - was right here; right in your Soul's vibration? What if the Song of your Soul was the vibration of the creation power of this universe?

While I was in the process of writing this book, I had the impulse to learn more about *Hildegard von Bingen*, a sounding mystic of the 11th century. I didn't immediately act on my intuition and only ordered a book about her visions in the later stages of writing - to be precise - I ordered a book about her visions when I put together this last chapter. The book arrived and I was somehow excited and nervous. I carried the package upstairs into my apartment and while opening the amazon wrapping, I heard inside my spirit: *"Read page 34."* I took the book, opened page 34, and began to read: *"Just as a circle embraces all that is within it, so does the Godhead embrace all. [...] God hugs you. You are encircled by the arms of the mystery of God."* I broke out into tears, and I literally sank on my knees to the floor. My heart was bursting wide open for what Hildegard von Bingen described here was *my* exact experience, too. What she saw and felt in her visions was what I had just put together for this chapter

- the Divine being a sacred spiral, pulling us ever deeper into its sounding embrace.

Now, to be completely honest; writing a book isn't an easy. Certainly not a book about the depth of the Soul with a mission to transform people's life and help them heal. It's comparable to birthing a baby. I had to summon the vibration of my Soul day after day after day to stay focused on my assigned task. I'm not gonna lie to you, I had days of great flow, and days where I felt stuck, days of feeling the Divine was writing through me, and days where I asked myself, *"How am I ever gonna finish this chapter?"* Hildegard's prophetic words came like an undeniable divine confirmation and were like balm for my heart. I could feel the tangible presence of the Divine Mother in the room reading her phrases. I couldn't believe I had made the same experiences as she did. She felt like an older sister to me – a mystic that had walked the path before. *Yes, the Divine hugs us, yes, it surrounds us, yes it is like an everlasting, sacred spiral of sounding grace pulling us in.*

Finding yourself in the sacred spiral day by day

When I wrote this last chapter, I woke up one morning and the first thing I heard inside my spirit was, *'Let me draw you deeper into the Sacred Spiral of the Divine, don't let yourself be drawn into spirals of darkness.'* I was a bit shaken up and started to reflect. There *are* spirals of light *and* of darkness. With every move we make, we can decide for or against our SoundingSoul. With every word we say, we have a choice. With every thought, we are sending an encoded vibration. The deeper we enter the realm of the Soul, the more clearly we see. In the presence of increasing light, our shadow becomes more apparent, too. We can't be mystic healers bestowing grace upon the land without deep inner work.

The path of the Soul is a path of truth. We need to allow our Soul to take us into ever deeper layers so that we can meet what drives us and come back to practical service; the natural state of the Soul. We are meant to make a difference in this world – and we might or might not be recognized for it. Maybe you are called to meditate and sound prayers for your neighborhood every day, balancing your entire community with the sounding grace you're generating. Maybe no one will ever know that it is your prayers that keep your neighborhood balanced in peace and harmony with little or no crimes. Maybe you are meant to bring together multitudes, healing many by sounding the Song of the Mother, Maybe you are called to form new communities, sounding into existence a New Earth. Only you will know the answer.

Each day, we have the choice of either becoming a sounding vessel of grace, or remaining victims, staying in a state of woundedness, using our past, present, or future to justify stagnation. We can spiral down not only into victimhood, but also blame, self-pity, bitterness, unforgiveness, self-sabotage, manipulation, addiction, gossip, negativity, criticism, and self-destruction because we might feel the need to take vengeance, or simply because we think it is our right to feel the way we do. There are spirals of pride, (spiritual) arrogance, entitlement, and self-abusive, as well as a bottomless feeling of unworthiness, and mistrust in oneself. The many, belittling dark spirals want to keep us in denial of the presence of our divine vibration, and are trying to pull us away from the sounding presence of the Mother in ouf Soul, convincing us that we have the right to dwell on these dark emotions.

Now – I don't want to live in these energies. Do you? Luckily, we always have an alternative: *The glory of the sacred, sounding Spiral of the Soul!* This SACRED SPIRAL exceeds any negativity and makes each of the many dark mazes we might have chosen in the past go up in smoke. It is the spiral of glorious, nourishing, all-encompassing, ever-sounding grace of the Mother. It is the sacred spiral, irresistible in beauty, consisting of sounding, cosmic light; devoted to the good of all of creation. It is the sacred spiral of the Soul, filled with visions, clarity, and abundance. *The sacred, sounding Spiral of the Soul evokes healing, empowerment, and blossoming* in all areas of life. We are invited to live in this sounding divine reality and exchange it for the many, meaningless little dark spirals we might have gotten caught in.

If you find yourself stuck in a victim mentality luring you to live in the past, not able to let go, forgive, and move on, *then pray.* Sing your prayers. Dance them. Movement and Sound will help you to shake yourself out of negativity, step by step. If you feel you are your own prisoner, blaming others for what you're facing, *pray*. Sound. Sing a song of releasing. Sound a mantra of letting go. With all my heart, I urge you to pray like you're crazy. Sound your prayers like your life depended on it so you might realize again the divine sounding strength inside of you that will pour down like a mighty waterfall, right into your being. Activate your *Soulstar* (the energetic center of your Soul a few inches above your Crown Chakra) by simply sounding or speaking the SoulMantram. The divine vibration of your SoulStar has the power to pull you out of any dark spirals back into the glory of your divine origin in the blink of an eye. Simply focus your attention on your Soul and speak/sound this SoulMantram:

I AM THE SOUL.
I AM THE LIGHT DIVINE
I AM LOVE
I AM WILL
I AM FIXED DESIGN.

(The truth of the SoulMantram is reflected in the *SoulStarLights*. Learn more about them on my website and get your own SoulStarLight as a visible, physical reminder of the Divine Vibration you are, expanding in all directions, sparkling like a star.)

SoundSouljournal:

Maybe you'd like to reflect on your 'typical' dark spirals that are pulling you into lower vibrations from time to time. Activate the Song of your Soul through sounding and enter the sacred spiral of Source, lovingly calling you back into peace.

Surrendering your baby plans

JUST A LITTLE WHILE AGO, I sat together with my Guides and SoundingSoul in an afternoon meeting. I do this regularly, usually in the mornings, checking in with my higher self (another word for your SoundingSoul). It's like being in an open conversation of *"Hey, what's up Universe?", "What is this day supposed to look like?", "What are the next steps you want me to take in order to be of service?"* I love those meetings. And often, *very* often, my Guides and SoundingSoul are bringing forth guidance I don't quite expect, catapulting me out of any in-the-box-thinking there might be.

So here I was sitting, in a meditative receptive space when all of a sudden I heard a clear phrase inside myself: "It is time to surrender your baby plans. Stop playing small. It is time to be bold, dream big and manifest what you have known for a long time."

Now, you have to know, I have been a gold digger for my purpose and calling for a long time. I kind of thought I had found it; I was in the belief that I knew what I had to do in order to fulfill my calling. Training the SoundPriestesses of our days and helping them step into their calling by launching my SoundPriestess Mystery School is part of it. And yes, helping as many people as possible to come back to the Song of the Mother, activating their own throat chakras and sounding healing into their lives and the world through all kinds of courses and programs I would create in the future. Isn't that pretty big already? I mean, common!

What I saw though, that afternoon, was an entire other level of what I had pictured so far. In the blink of an eye, my SoundingSoul blew over my ideas of how I thought my calling would play out in the near and far future dispelling my small minded thinking in an instant. I had a vision which exceeded anything I could possibly have imagined and again I heard: *"It is time for you to throw your baby plans overboard and follow the course of your Soul. Set the sails and get ready."*

Now, at this very moment, I will not share with you what I saw. I will tell you when I am there. Let me just say, there was no more room for baby plans, for plans that seem manageable. This vision stretched me into the endless possibilities of the Soul, born out of faith. What I saw was FAR BIGGER than what I had allowed myself to dream about these past years. You know what's funny though? I had seen this already when I was a teenager. I saw myself doing exactly what I was doing in this vision when I was about 18. *Ha!* The advantage of the passion and enthusiasm of our youth is priceless! Time to come back to hunger for adventure we had back then and combine it with the wisdom we since gained.

I want you to take a moment today or latest sometime this week (schedule it into your calendar) where you sit with your SoundingSoul and ask: *"What are some of my baby plans ? Where did I subconsciously submit to baby plans because I thought it was the more sensible thing to do? Where, my SoundingSoul, are you calling me to level up into the royal plans of the Divine and set the sails?"*

SoundSoulJournal

Take some time to sit with these questions, letting your SoundingSoul speak to you.

The Song of the Phoenix

WHAT MIGHT HELP IN THIS PROCESS IS THE LEGEND OF THE PHOENIX . Ancient legends tell us about Phoenix; a magical, large bird, radiantly glowing, colored in beautiful reds, purples, and yellows, reminding us of a sunrise or crackling fire. Sometimes, old paintings show the Phoenix with a halo, illuminating his surroundings. After having lived for several hundred years, he builds a special nest with a unique purpose, choosing the finest aromatic woods and igniting it with a single clap of his wings, so the legend says. The Phoenix is consumed by the flames, his glorious feathers reduced to ashes. Most astonishing in the Phoenix legend is that the bird builds his own death bed, putting it on fire and burning himself to death. Thankfully, that's not the end of the story as the most unexpected is yet to happen: from the pile of ashes, a young, powerful, glorious Phoenix arises, *"singing the Song of resurrection and rebirth"* (Phoenix Sayings and Quotes).

The mystic symbolism and timeless meaning of the Phoenix legend seems almost inexhaustible. Let's begin with sacred, organic-universal cycles. The ancient bird undergoes the eternal cycle of life, death, and rebirth/ resurrection. As one cycle is completed, he sets himself on fire to be transformed into the new, the evolutionary inevitable next phase. He is often portrayed with blue, clear eyes - a symbol of a *seer*, prophesying the ever-developing stages of creation. He senses when the time has come to transition into the new, gathers the finest woods, claps his wings, and lets himself be consumed by the flames of divine destruction, chaos, turmoil, disguising the most sacred process of it all: a process of *restructuring*. He offers the present, past, and future to the fire of transformation and rises from the ashes to new, evolved dimensions of life.

The Phoenix bird *re-member-ed* his SoundingSoul to such an extent that in the moment of building his death-nest, the fire simply takes on another form, shifting from the fire *within* to the fire *without*. It is the same fire the Phoenix cultivated inside throughout many centuries. He lived in the reality of his Soul, made tangible through the sacred Song he sings. The Phoenix lives and dies and rises to new life for one and one purpose only: *To be one with Divine Source, fulfilling divine purpose furthermore.*

There is a beautiful, simple tradition in both of my ascendant lines of this incarnation. Whenever someone is dying, the family gathers around the person and sings. Songs of comfort, songs of life, songs of nature, and the eternal dimension to ease the dying person's journey into the next dimension. How wonderful to transition like that, surrounded by your loved ones, singing and sounding the cosmic reality within. My grandmother, who was a very active, optimistic woman, dedicated to bringing light to the lives of many, left her body at the age of ninety-seven. She sang her entire life. Her favorite song that I played and sang with her many times goes something like this: *Those who love God will be like the sun that rises in its splendor.* She had no easy life at all and it brings tears to my eyes each time this melody arises in my heart. A few days before she passed, she continuously mentioned she was hearing astounding beautiful music. Only – that there was no music playing in her room or anywhere close. She couldn't understand why no one seemed to notice the divine sounding beauty she heard. I wholeheartedly believe my grandmother was hearing the Sounds of Heaven, calling her Soul into the everlasting embrace of God.

The Phoenix is ready for his death ceremony because he was singing the Song of his Soul *all his life*. He can entrust himself to the flames of transformation because he tasted, ate, and was sustained by the substance the Song of the Mother is made of: *divine, trembling, nutritious, glorious Sound*. A Sound *existential* for life. A Sound reminding us of who we are. The Phoenix tapped into its powers every day. Consumed by its beauty and unconditional love, he became one with his sounding, inner nature, courageously stepping into the next phase of cosmic evolution. *Not my will but thy will - surrendering to the divine Sound within.*

Cycling through the realm of the Soul

THE SOUND OF OUR SOUL evolves and flows – it expands and spirals eternally into ever deeper layers of the Cosmic Song. The twelve different stages we've explored in this book are like stars or planets in the galaxies and invite us to come back any time just as the planets travel around the sun and each other continuously. Don't shy away from regular revisits nor consider repetition a sign of weakness. The path of the Soul is infinite and multidimensionally cyclic. We need to travel through the inner, cosmic spiral and visit each of the spheres of the Soul again and again. We simply spiral deeper and deeper, like the layers of an onion.

Our journey touched on twelve fundamental phases of a Soul journey on Earth: We saw how all life is Sound (1); we discovered that our real identity is of divine untouchable nature (2), we plunged into conscious silence (3), and explored the necessity to be continuously engaged in deep inner healing and personal shadow work, tending to our inner child (4). We experienced Self-Sounding as an essential practice that bridges the transcendent and physical, generating a direct experience of the Divine (5). Once we become aware of the Song of our Soul, we need to understand its message and *live* by its purpose (6). We looked at the importance of reflecting and radiating the Song of our Soul through and from our body-temples, treating them with care and respect (7); we dove into sacred sexuality (8), and our relationship to the Earth and her Song (9). We discovered that expressing our divine vibration through our professional life based on practical service is not only fulfilling but a natural consequence of following the Song of our Soul (10), so we can furthermore step into the aquarian calling by becoming modern-day mystics, selflessly bestowing healing upon the thirsty land (11), and surrendering to the fire within, the Song of the Mother, the fire of the Divine Feminine, allowing her to transform our baby plans into the bold, divine adventures our SoundingSoul came to this planet for. All twelve phases are part of the journey, equipping us to rise to ever-deeper, ever-evolving, ever-regenerative, ever-expanding new cycles of life into ever deepening layers of the Soul, radiating more and more of the omni-present, sounding glory of the Divine *throughout all eons of time.*

Cycle back into any of these phases regularly. It will pay off!

Entering the Sounding Gates of your Soul - every day

Your Soul will guide you to whatever is best at any given moment. Trust her guidance. Trust her gentle pull. Trust her Song. If you are serious about walking a spiritual path, I'd love to encourage you to set aside a minimum of thirty minutes each day to get to know the sounding treasures within. *(For best results, I recommend thirty minutes in the morning after getting up, and thirty minutes in the evening before going to sleep).*

Every day, your Soul is longing for you to enter the Divine Reality through her glorious, sounding gates. Don't hesitate. Walk into the realm of the Soul, the doors are wide open; the sounding presence of the Divine ready to embrace you. You are here on this planet because of your Soul's cosmic agreement. It is time to rise to the true Soul adventures of your Soul. It is time to burn the old, the outdated, the boring, the numbing, the belittling, and rise from the ashes like the Phoenix to the glory of your Soul. Rise, ye Daughters of Jerusalem, rise ye Daughters of New Earth. Sing the Song of the Mother! The Mother is calling. The Mother is calling all her children to remember who they are. You are alive at this point in time of humanity for a specific task that only you can fulfill. It is time to *sound*. It is time to *sing* and share your divine essence. It is time to manifest what you hear ringing and vibrating within. Become that bell. Become that bell of divine vibration and birth what you meant to birth, into the physical.

We're called to drop into our sounding essence right now, resting assured that we are never alone, nurtured by Sounding Source holding us all in its all-encompassing embrace. From this place of truth, let's sing the Song of the Soul, *leading many home*, home into the very heart of God.

THANK YOU

Thanks be to the Mother.
Thanks be to her Song.
Thanks be to the Father.
To whom I belong.

Thanks to The Beloved
Beloved One indeed.
Thank you for your guidance
Ever so concrete.

Thanks Divine Vibration
Buzzing within me
Thank you, SoundingSoul
For helping me to see.

Thank you Universe
For helping me to birth
These lines of sounding power
Calling forth our one true worth.

Thanks to you, my reader
For opening your heart
Become a golden weaver
For Heaven on Earth play your part.

SoundSoulJournal

First Chapter ~ All is Sound

How did I feel during the "I am part of the Cosmic Song" SoundMeditation?

N/A

Am I experiencing myself as part of the Cosmic Song?

Sometimes during meditation and connecting with nature.

How would my life be different if I perceived it through my ears versus my eyes?

Non judgement. Sound vibrations felt. Everything louder and more tangible. Feel more connected to nature. Heightens my intuition. Noticing far more different sounds at once which normally go unnoticed. Perception + clarity.

What is my relationship to my(speaking) voice?

Sometimes frustrated when I dont say what I truly feel.

Like my voice, can be rather fast and tends to interrupt people sometimes.

Change it to fit who I speak to.

Excitable, nervous, loving, earthy, clear, resonant. Need to work on grounding.

How do I feel about falling in love with my voice and ground it, anchoring it in my body, my truth?

Very positive its something I desire to do. I'm ready! I am already starting to love my voice. I just need to let others truly hear it for what it is.

Do I mostly see myself as a separate entity from the cosmic Whole? If so, where do I feel this perception comes from?

No I see mysey as connected into everything. But sometimes I need to remind mysey so when I get caug up in my busy life. This perception comes from programming and our beley systems.

Further Reflections:

Second Chapter ~ Sounding Identity ~ Who am I?

How did my sense of identity shift throughout the Identity Exercise?

The original statements felt like I was just a factual piece of paper with no real life. It felt flat, almost non existent. In fact pretty dull and miserable.

Afterwords I felt free, stepping into who I truly am. Excited and happy to be me in its entirety. Joyous! Free from labels, identity and just be another little minion on earth for the elites!

Further Reflections:

Third Chapter ~ Conscious Silence

Let's practice some silence right now! Turn off all devices, sit with awareness of your spine, feel the ground beneath your feet and breathe. Deeply. Count on 4 on your inhale and count on 4 on your exhale. Pause in between in-& exhale for a moment. Do this for 5 minutes.

7 Day Conscious Silence Practice Challenge. Practice the breathing exercise above every day.

Day 1, Date, Time & my experience:

Day 2, Date, Time & my experience:

Day 3, Date, Time & my experience:

Day 4, Date, Time & my experience:

Day 5, Date, Time & my experience:

Day 6, Date, Time & my experience:

Day 7, Date, Time & my experience:

Congratulations! You made it through the 7 Day Conscious Silence Breathing Challenge!

Further Reflections:

Fourth Chapter ~ What inside of you is longing to be heard?

What situation recently triggered me?

Can I connect with my inner child and come closer to the root cause of why I felt the way I did?

Would I like to schedule a session with a trusted spiritual Mentor to go deeper into my own healing?

Further Reflections:

Fifth Chapter ~ The Power of SelfSounding

How do I feel if I consciously hum for 5 minutes?

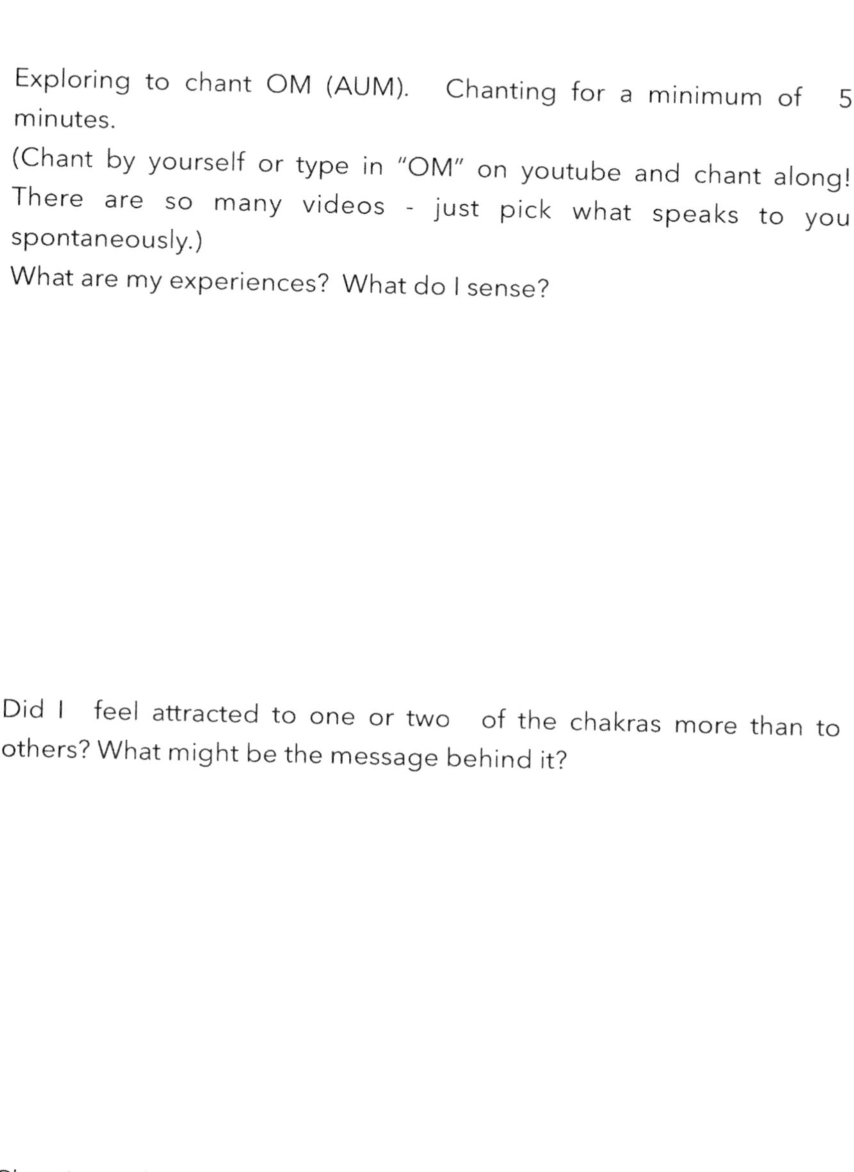

Exploring to chant OM (AUM). Chanting for a minimum of 5 minutes.
(Chant by yourself or type in "OM" on youtube and chant along! There are so many videos - just pick what speaks to you spontaneously.)
What are my experiences? What do I sense?

Did I feel attracted to one or two of the chakras more than to others? What might be the message behind it?

Chanting their seed mantras. What do I sense when sounding a seed-mantra? Which ones would I like to explore at this stage of my life?

Do I experience energetic leaks in my life? Which chakras do the leaks correlate with? Would I like to call back your energy and unplug? How could you manage your energy more consciously?

Have I heard my Soul's sacred syllable? Would I like to sit in meditation and open myself to receive it?

What might be a personalized mantra that would help me transform or heal a certain area of my life right now?

Further Reflections:

Sixth Chapter ~ The Song of your Calling

What experience did you make reading through this meditative text of encountering your immortal Soul?

What do I feel might be my Soul's calling?

Further Reflections:

Seventh Chapter ~ The Song of the Body ~ Sounding Temple

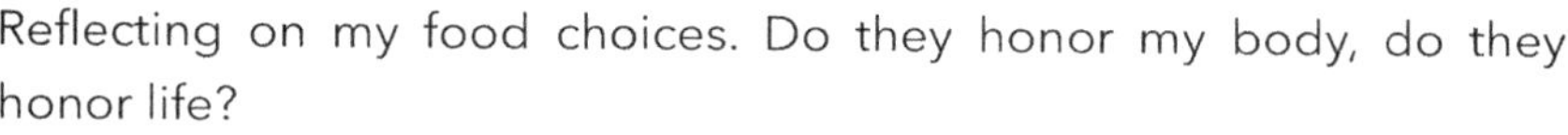

Reflecting on my food choices. Do they honor my body, do they honor life?

How do I feel after my meals? What would I like to change or explore?

How could I lovingly tend to my body on a daily basis?

Would I like to explore yoga in my life?

Further Reflections:

Eighth Chapter ~ The Song of Sacred Sexuality

Transcending sexual shame:

Breathe deeply a few times. Breathing in fully, sighing it out completely. And again. Breathe deep into your belly and exhale completely. Now write down any sexual memory that feels in any way uncomfortable. Write down anything that arises. What were your family's beliefs around sex? How did your parents speak or didn't speak about it? What were your personal first sexual explorations and encounters? What were your parents' reactions to you discovering your sexuality? Write down anything related to your sexuality that comes to your awareness. Simply be there with any feeling that is bubbling up. Allow it to be felt. Locate in your body where you are sensing the emotion and connect to the part of you that experienced what you remember. What beliefs got created in you in these moments? What are you ready to let go of?

My Reflections:

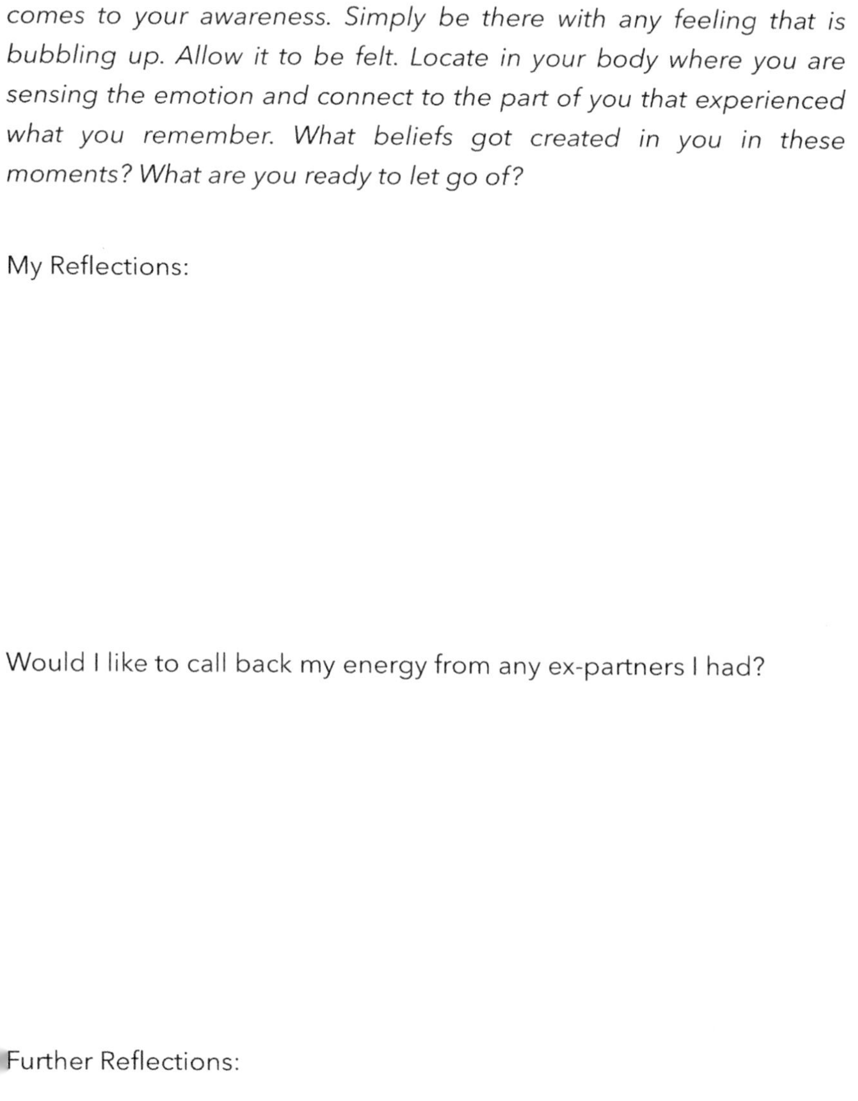

Would I like to call back my energy from any ex-partners I had?

Further Reflections:

Ninth Chapter ~ The Song of Gaia ~ Living in the sacred frequency of Earth

How could I reestablish a deep relationship with nature, with Mother Earth?

Sitting outside on the ground. Let your entire being be flooded with sounding love. Breathe in your inherent divinity and let go of worries and stress. Breathe in your cosmically sounding essence and breathe out any feeling of depletion or overwhelm. Know that you are loved no matter what; know that you are enough. Take your time and sink into this truth. And when you feel really grounded and connected, ask this question:

'What is my relationship to Earth? How can I contribute to the healing of the planet? Please sing to me Gaia. Sing to me your ancient Song' Just listen. Receive. And when you're filled and nourished to the brim, act.

My reflections:

Further Reflections:

Tenth Chapter ~ Practical Service ~ Manifesting my Divine Vibration

What do I most love in this life?
What could I do for hours and hours without getting tired?
What fills my heart with joy and a feeling of overflowing gratitude?
What touches me so deeply that it makes me cry?

What are my SoulGifts?

What could my practical Service look like?

What is my relationship to abundance?

What is my relationship to gold & silver?

Further Reflections:

Eleventh Chapter ~ The Song of the Aquarian Age ~ Bestowing Healing upon the Land

Where in your life do I feel betrayed? Is it possible that a divine intelligence orchestrated this betrayal for a reason much bigger than me? So I could grow and mature into your potential? Is it possible that there is a higher force behind my life, bringing together the necessary pieces of a puzzle whose size I do not know yet? How do deal with betrayal in my life? Am I able to keep my heart open, trust and improvise if life wasn't playing out the way I wanted? How anchored am I in the truth of my Soul, knowing in any situation that my life is in the hands of God - not of men?

My Reflections:

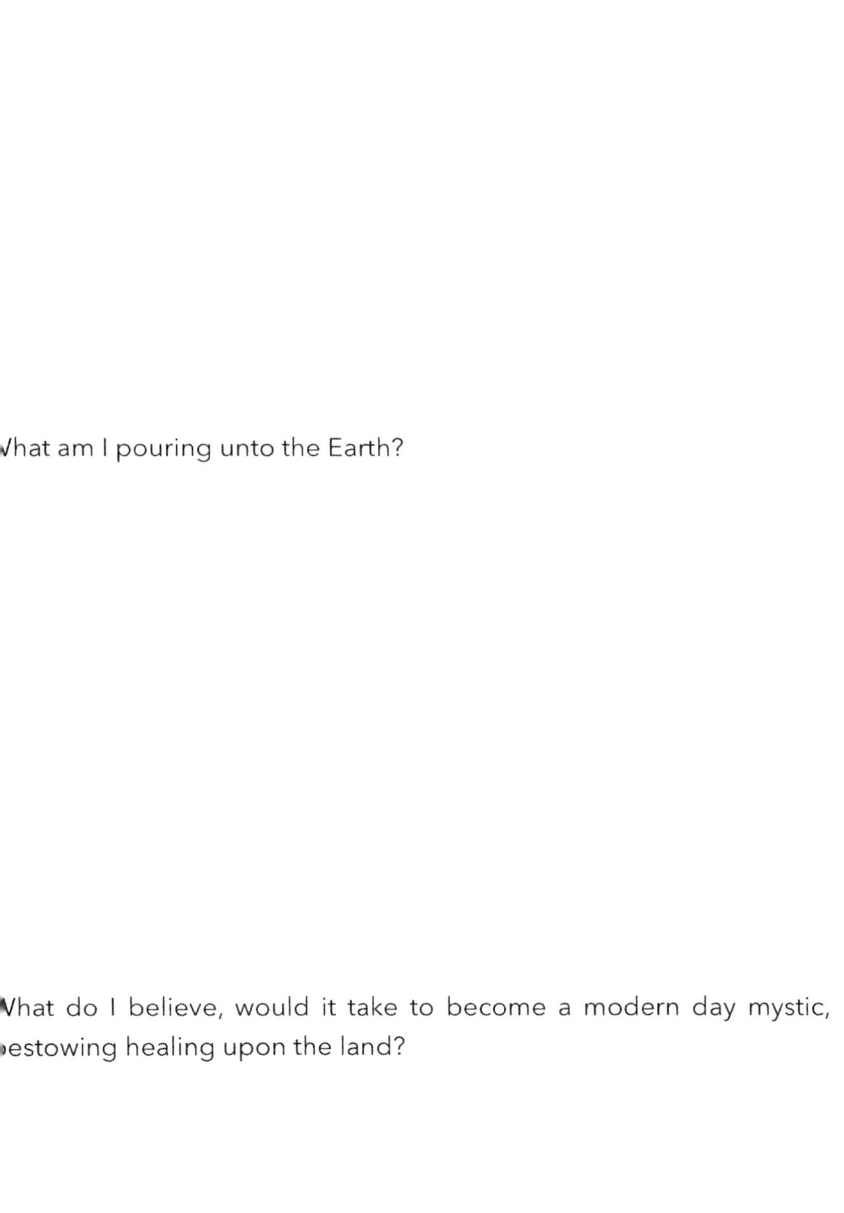

What am I pouring unto the Earth?

What do I believe, would it take to become a modern day mystic, bestowing healing upon the land?

Further Reflections:

Twelfth Chapter ~ The Song of Mother ~ Entering the Sacred Spirals of the Divine Feminine

How do I experience the Song of the Mother? How do I feel chanting the Adi-Shakti Mantra?

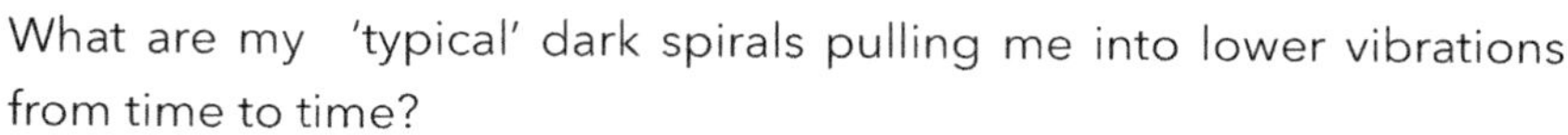

What are my 'typical' dark spirals pulling me into lower vibrations from time to time?

SOUNDING PRAYERS:

Engaging in activating the Song of your Soul through sounding prayer and entering the sacred spiral of Source, lovingly calling me back into pea**ce.**

Have I ever sounded my prayers? Danced them? Would I like to try?

What are some of my baby plans ? Where did I subconsciously submit to baby plans because I thought it was the more sensible thing to do? Where, my SoundingSoul, are you calling me to level up into the royal plans of the Divine and set the sails?

Further Reflections:

Bibliography

"Adi Shakti Mantra Meditation Meaning - Kundalini Mantra." wakening State, Awakening State, 2020, https://www.awakeningstate.com/spiritual-awakening/adi-shakti-nantra/.

"Calling on Adi Shakti." Sikh Dharma International, Sikh Dharma nternational, 27 January 2017, https://www.sikhdharma.org/woman-dignity-divinity-merge-ogether-2/.

"Deaf People Can "Feel" Music." WebMD, WebMD, 28 November 001, https://www.webmd.com/a-to-z-guides/news/20011128/deaf-eople-can-feel-music

Delamora, Transformational Experiences, Inspirational Quotes https://www.delamora.life/inspirational-quotes-music-sound

"Genesis 45." BibleGateway, BibleGateway, 2016,

https://www.biblegateway.com/passage/?search=Genesis+45&version=ESV.

Massachusetts Institute of Technology. "New Devices Aid Deaf People By Translating Sound Waves To Vibrations." ScienceDaily, ScienceDaily, 2 March 2009, https://www.sciencedaily.com/releases/2009/02/090227112311.htm.

"Phoenix Sayings and Quotes." Wise Old Sayings, Wise Old Sayings, 2000-2020, https://www.wiseoldsayings.com/phoenix-quotes/.

"Plastic Debris in the Open Ocean." PNAS, National Academy of Sciences, 13 June 2013, https://www.pnas.org/content/111/28/10239.

About the Author

M*aalii Magdalene Bey* is dedicated to birthing and building a New Earth based on the universal laws of harmony and love. Originally trained as a professional opera singer and classically trained pianist/musician, her spiritual path called her to work with the transformative powers of Sound in the field of personal Healing, Empowerment & Transformation of the individual and our planet. *Maalii Magdalene* works 1:1 with people in *SoundHealing Embodiment Sessions* and has recorded about five hundred personal Sound-Readings for people all over the globe. She offers live workshops, online classes, and extensive *Soul-Path Frequency Readings*. Maalii's *Sound-Priestess Mystery School* will be launched in 2022. To learn more, please visit her website www.soundingsouls.com.

Printed in Great Britain
by Amazon

82225900R00109